DISILLUSIONED

WHEN YOU GET LOST FOLLOWING JESUS

MELANIE J. SAWARD

Ark House Press
PO Box 1722, Port Orchard, WA 98366 USA
PO Box 1321, Mona Vale NSW 1660 Australia
PO Box 318 334, West Harbour, Auckland 0661 New Zealand
arkhousepress.com

Cataloguing in Publication Data:
Title: Disillusioned
ISBN: 978-0-6489380-4-0 (pbk)
Subjects: Church; Christian Living;
Other Authors/Contributors: Saward, Melanie J.

Design by initiateagency.com

ACKNOWLEDGEMENTS

Thank you to my husband Josh, who has always been by my side. You've listened to every painful and ridiculous thought I've had. You've given me grace and patience even when my adventures have made you nervous. Thank you for trusting me.

My dearest Leela. Will I ever stop learning from you?! I hope that I make you proud and set an example that leads you to a deeper faith in Jesus.

To Pastor Ben & Emily Higgins & Pastors' Geoff & Lee Blight - Thank you for being such a significant part of the healing process for me. Being apart of your church family has done so much to restore my hope in the Body of Christ.

Liz Swanson, again for being such an exceptional editor that encourages and challenges with grace and wisdom.

Gugu Bhebhe. I just want to thank you for being such an exceptional woman. Articulate, insightful and profound. Thank you for supporting me in writing one of the hardest sections I've ever been lead to write.

CONTENTS

Loose Ends

Seekers of meaning. That's what we've been told we are. We humans, by our very nature, desperately seek meaning. Whether it's derived from daily, by being assured that our lives have purpose and value. Or the larger-scale kind of meaning, that seeks to make sense out of life and the universe. We may not always feel like we are constantly on a quest for meaning since much of our worldview is taught to us by our parents and childhood environments. It's often not until later in life that we are forced to clarify the meanings that were prescribed, if not to completely redefine them.

In essence, being a meaning-seeker is the internal desire to hang your hat on something worthwhile. I don't have a hat, nor do I have a place to hang hats. But I know what it feels like to want to rely on something that is stable and makes sense of everything around and in me.

The challenge with being a meaning-seeker is that there is so much opportunity for disappointment. Sometimes meaning is really hard to find. Sometimes our pursuit of meaning, leaves us with loose ends. And we don't like loose ends. And when you can't lock down a precise indestructible unable-to-make-holes-in-it meaning, you end up with a lot of loose ends. Of the little bit of sewing I have done in my lifetime, I learnt one thing very quickly. If you don't tie a knot at the end of the thread, it's going to come undone. And loose threads can unravel the whole project. Likewise, because of our inherent need for meaning, we don't handle things very well when something doesn't make sense. When threads link together and hold a garment in place, they seem complete. They have met their destiny. They are logically realised, and we feel at peace. But loose ends do not generally produce peace.

This is where disillusionment kicks in. This is what happens when we have an apparently irreconcilable loose end. We have a belief, and we have a reality that we are unable to attach or reattach. In some cases, this state of mind can collapse the foundations on which a person stands. In this state a person has no emotional safety to rely on and only confusion remains. Along with such uncertainty enters a myriad of symptoms that seem impossible to navigate.

In the last two years, I have found myself face to face with disillusionment a number of times. Some were small, and some were life impacting. I had to confront some really tough loose ends that were incredibly difficult to reconcile. Some of which would have led me to a very different path in my faith and long-term mental health. God gave me the wisdom via the leading of the Holy Spirit, to recognise disillusionment early and explore it personally as I waded through its waters. And I have emerged bone dry from those waters. However, like most people I assumed that disillusionment was an inescapable reality rather than another means through which Jesus can demonstrate His saving grace, and deepen our relationship with Him.

Disillusionment is very influential. Today's society is emotionally, psychologically and spiritually impoverished by disillusionment. There are very few areas of life in which people can put their trust. And that makes for a lot of loose ends. And the list of institutions and ideologies to mistrust grows daily. Everything from politicians, to the royal family and religious institutions. Even science has lost its superior status, as people realise that the information is in constant flux or that scientific studies are often driven by big businesses with robust agendas.

Many believers seemed trapped by disillusionment. For some it seems easier to make permanent homes in this state of mind that was only ever meant to be temporary. The emergence of different Christian celebrities renouncing their faith, may indicate the heights at which disillusionment is present in Christian society. It's hard to say, since I don't know the full story of those believers and how they came to renounce their faith. Though persistent disillusionment could certainly cause you to walk away from faith.

The most obvious disillusionment can be seen in the copious numbers of people leaving traditional churches, never to return again. My assertion is that there are more people leaving churches today on account of disillusionment than 'offence'. I have heard hundreds of messages, in which Pastors and leaders blame offence as the cause for people walking away from faith. Yes, offence does play a part…but not all the time.

But there are disillusioned people attending churches right now who are frequently on the verge of reconsidering their allegiances. They might be the people who Pastors point to as 'uncommitted'. They may be the ones who we are trying to engage, because they are the hardest to motivate. They may be the ones who turn up every couple of weeks, but don't seem to want to step any further.

Yes, the roots of disillusionment have been long standing and deep. Unfortunately, this is because our mistrust has been validated. We do find out that some politicians are dodgy. We do find out that Pastors keep secret sins. We do find out that the big companies are syphoning off employees well earned income. But the disillusionment that often eventuates out of such realities, is a truly unhealthy place to reside. Without intervention or interruption, disillusionment can become a haunting state of mind.

Therefore, my hope in writing this book is to bring some clarity to the way forward from disillusionment. Healing is possible, and it is probable… when we understand exactly what disillusionment is and how it operates. Secondly, this book will assist believers in considering disillusionment in reflection upon God and His sovereignty. Thirdly, I hope it encourages all believers to have understanding, kindness and patience with those around you who are currently enduring disillusionment.

Final thoughts before we start this journey; this is not a science. I know what has worked for me, and that is what I intend to share. Everything I have learnt has come through reflection, discussion with trusted friends, and contemplating scripture and prayer. Whilst I have high hopes that this book could facilitate freedom, I know that it's not going to do that for everyone. And so I pray that you would receive what has always intended to be my effort to help, discard what doesn't resonate, but continue to seek God on this journey to wholehearted freedom.

CHAPTER 1

Seeing past the fog

Twenty-five years prior to the Titanic, two steamships of the White Star Line collided 350 miles east of Sandy Hook in New Jersey. Twelve people died with almost twenty injured as a result of the incident occurring at 5:25 pm on Thursday 19th May 1887.

The SS Britannic was on the second day of its journey to Liverpool, the SS Celtic was arriving into New York. The culprit of the collision? A dense fog. Reports suggest that the SS Britannic's fog bell had been ringing and the SS Celtic's fog bell was ringing, yet only the SS Celtic's bell was heard after the collision. But the fog itself was masking the direction of the fog bells making the collision imminent. The SS Celtic hit the SS Britannic three times leaving a large hole underneath the ship. A panic ensued on board the SS Britannic, with passengers scurrying towards the rescue boats until the captain intervened with a pistol as a warning, preventing the men from jumping the queue and allowing the women and children to board first.

It's sometimes hard for us to grasp how a natural almost daily occurrence like fog could cause such panic and devastation. When I'm informed at an airport that my plane is delayed because of a fog, I am sincerely put out wondering how our modern technology is unable to account for such matters. But in this historical example, the fog created so much confusion.

Firstly, the fog made it impossible for two very large steamships to see each other. According to records, the SS Britannic was 138 metres long and the SS Celtic was 133 metres long. To put this size into perspective, an American football field is 109 metres long. Both vessels superseded the length of a football field, and yet were still unable to be seen by each other in the fog. Secondly, though it can be hard to find information that confirms the loudness of a ship's fog bell at that time in history, today's reports suggest that a fog bell can be heard from between 1.2 km (¾ mile) and 11km (7 miles) away. And yet the fog's density was the only factor causing both fog bells to be virtually undetectable by each other. Thirdly, it caused such panic that people lost all sense of order, causing a man with a pistol to be the most reasonable person onboard. In other words, the threat to life was the only way calmness could be established on the boat.

It is sufficient to say that fog can be pretty scary. The scariest part about an incident like this is the unknown. You just wouldn't have any clue what is on the other side of that fog. And how could you adequately prepare for what might be ahead?

This is what disillusionment feels like. Disillusionment is like a fog of confusion. Everything that was clear and understandable, is now uncertain. Disappointment and broken expectations cause the fog to settle. Whilst fear, the threat to stability and confusion numb any wise rhetoric. The confusion can be so pervading that a way forward can seem insurmountable. And the disillusioned person's capacity to hear signs of hope are greatly nullified. Though your logical mind may try to convince you otherwise, in that mental and emotional state it can feel safer to stay still in a perpetual state of emotional detachment. Since the only viable alternative seems to be doing absolutely anything possible to jump off that ship...even if it hurts people on the way.

DISILLUSIONMENT UNDER A MICROSCOPE

Disillusionment is the realisation that things are not at all as you thought they were. It's when it suddenly dawns on you that life doesn't work as you had been told, or had believed it worked. It's the fact that you could have been so wrong about something, to the point that you are genuinely confused and shocked by it. This new thing you have seen is something that can never be unseen, nor can it be ignored. Disillusionment is the emotional and psychological equivalent of a 'check-mate' in chess.

For some, disillusionment is temporary and passes with time. And yet others can have long standing disillusionment that corrupts their entire perception, dominating their whole life experience especially when that belief was underpinning their worldview and sense of meaning. At its core, it is a loss of psychological and emotional safety.

In my first experience with disillusionment, the new information caused my whole life to go on hold for five hours. In those hours I was unable to even form intelligible words, as my mind bounced from one incomplete thought to another incomplete thought. My mind and emotions were in a frenzy. Yes, it does sound a lot like shock. And often that is how disillusionment will start. Whilst that first occasion passed, many more would arise that would vary between momentary disillusioning thoughts and full blown disillusionment that lasted months if not years.

So, why is disillusionment so devastating?

"THERE MAY BE SOMETHING THERE THAT WASN'T THERE BEFORE…"

When Belle is held captive by a raging beast, in a dark castle in the classic Disney movie, 'Beauty and The Beast', never in her wildest of dreams would she think that she might have affection toward this terrifying man that is holding her against her will. And so, she belts out this sensational number, "There may be something there that wasn't there before" to describe her eyes being opened to a new positive possibility. Rather than a lifetime trapped in fear, she sees that she might live with some sense of joy that this beast is not so beastlike after all.

Naturally as meaning-seekers, finding new meaning is the equivalent of being enlightened. To be shown a better alternative is akin to a fantasy being actualised. It's euphoric. We are filled with hope at new possibilities. And we begin reconstructing our lives around these new exciting ideas that have earned our trust. That's how I felt when I first realised that God was indeed real. It was like seeing in colour after only ever seeing black and white. We might get nostalgic for black and white in photos, but imagine if black and white was all you ever saw? I suddenly feel rather sympathetic to dogs.

Unfortunately, not every new possibility is worthy of foundational status. The truth is the concept of disillusion first begins with illusion. The new possibilities of thinking and experiencing, that we were so excited about aren't necessarily rooted in truth. Admittedly, sometimes illusion is inevitable like in the case of childhood. During our formative years certain illusions develop out of survival and protection, most easily seen in the case of trauma.

But as the word implies, illusion is not reality, although it may appear to be. Illusions help us feel safe. But unfortunately, they are a hybrid reality because in every illusion there is usually an element of truth. This is what makes it seem so believable. Giving yourself fully to an illusion is where the trouble really begins. Especially when we begin to forfeit discernment in the face of them. Caution is dispelled when an illusion has gained your trust. Interestingly, you may have previously had an active role in the formation of that illusion, but at some point the illusion also takes a constructive role. In other words, it begins to shape you. The illusion reforms other existing ideas, and becomes a filter for all other ideas that you are confronted with. So, it plays an active role.

This also means that we can become a prisoner to our illusions. By nature, they demand submission and obedience. Because they are no longer external to our belief system, we are likely unquestioningly following their direction. Despite the fact that they aren't necessarily helpful, and they are not based completely in reality. An example might be the person who says, "immigrants are stealing our jobs". To the individual they wholeheartedly believe that jobs are capable of being stolen. For something to be stolen, the individual had to possess that thing in the first place. But this illusion further solidifies racist behaviour, and a victim mentality.

When we are forced to consider new information that threatens the security we find in our beliefs, it's like being robbed. Even if new information threatens our worldview, even if that worldview has been formed by osmosis, it's devastating to our sense of stability and demands new meaning be found.

Interestingly, this can be seen through the story of Siddhartha Gautama, also known as Buddha pre-his-supposed-enlightenment. The story of Buddha begins with a young man being born into a wealthy family, as a prince. In an effort to protect Buddha from the unsavoury hardship outside the Kingdom, they gave him all the luxury that a wealthy family could provide. You could say that his wealthy lifestyle was his illusion. However, at close to 30 years of age he ventured out past the kingdom walls only to observe the pain, suffering and degradation of some of the city's inhabitants. From those clusters of observations, the foundations of Buddhism were born. Buddha was attempting to bring meaning to the terrifying suffering that he saw. Thus, is the effect of disillusionment. That point at which Buddha saw something, guaranteed him that he would never be able to return to his earlier understanding of the meaning of life.

PHASES OF DISILLUSIONMENT

There seems to be a few phases to disillusionment that aren't necessarily in order.

A catalyst

> Usually there is some kind of event, whether it be a conversation, a vision, a discovery or any other multitude of occurrences that trigger the first stage of disillusionment. Something occurs for the individual to realise that something is conflicting with their previously held beliefs. It can be subtle, or it can be sudden. There is usually a point where it's impossible to ignore and the person essentially lets the walls down to confront the reality that they could have been wrong. For example, some of the events that precipitated various seasons of disillusionment in my own life include, a three-word response from a colleague, looking at a spreadsheet, a dream and a meeting.

Rumination and Processing

> This is where individual differences make a significant impact. People ultimately process in very different ways. In some cases, the person may retreat and not want to talk about the disillusionment, preferring to process their thoughts and feelings privately. For others, they may need to talk. It is important to note that there are risks with both. For the private processor there is the risk that they simply continue to rehearse the painful memories with little progress forward. For the talker, the risk is that they share their thoughts with the wrong people and the disillusionment worsens and continues to drift further into unhelpful assumptions. What is common to both, is the fact that it is increasingly difficult to cease the

ruminations toward the subject of the disillusionment. They will feel like it is pervading and constant, should they stay in the place where the disillusionment first occurred.

Resignation or Healing

Either the ruminations and processing leads to healing, or it leads to resignation. Healing is usually the intended outcome, if the person is able to recognise that there has been hurt that requires mending. Often those who are disillusioned assume that the change they are perceiving within themselves is just a change in viewpoint. They don't always recognise the emotional component to disillusionment. So their first assumption is not about a need for healing. Resignation, on the other hand, simply means that the person decides, whether actively or passively, that 'this is just the way it is'. It's not necessarily an acceptance, because they may still feel angry and upset at the source of their disillusionment. In resignation, a toxic narrative can remain.

It's important to note that it's very rare for a person to be completely healed, at least initially. Often various thoughts will come up that represent a residual disillusionment and the individual may have to continue to uncover the intricacies of their illusory belief system. These intricacies should be dealt with, if the person desires to successfully move forward. Paul writes in Hebrews 12:1

> "Therefore, since we are surrounded by such a huge crowd of witnesses to the life of faith, let us STRIP OFF EVERY WEIGHT THAT SLOWS US DOWN, especially the sin that so easily trips us up. And let us run with endurance the race God has set before us". (Hebrews 12:1 NLT, emphasis mine.)

Disillusionment may not strictly be a sin, but it definitely is a weight that slows us down. Even the minor thoughts of disillusionment are worthy of attention, if the intention is to run a race with endurance.

MOST COMMON AREAS FOR DISILLUSIONMENT

Disillusionment may arise in any realm of life where individual expectations can be generated. But in the Christian world there are some more common areas typically associated with disillusionment:

Marriage

The disillusionment around marriage is not only relating to the high divorce rates. It can also be because marriage has been so significantly elevated, particularly in churches, that spouses find themselves disillusioned when they realise that it isn't the beacon of companionship or sexuality that they were promised. The addition of children also significantly changes the dynamics of marriage, leading people to disillusioning thoughts.

Church

Church disillusionment is rampant and multi-layered. There is the disillusionment as leaders disappoint through indiscretions. And then there is the more national and global indiscretions of pastors and ministers and priests who have been found to be perpetrators of abuse through enquiries like Australia's Royal Commission into Institutional Responses to Child Sexual Abuse. There is the disillusionment that emerges as a result of high-level conflict in church. Whilst most recognise that church conflict is somewhat a normal part of church life, members are often shocked by the severe fallout and extremely unloving behaviours that emerge as a result of church conflict.

Many are often disillusioned by the experience of burn out that they either experience directly, or by others close to them. And finally, some are simply disillusioned by the idea that church is the answer'. They have been told to 'go to church', as a religious command. But in that time they may not have seen the personal impact from such commands.

Scripture

Many Christians are highly disillusioned by issues in scripture. If they are even able to articulate these issues in the first place, they often find that they are unable to talk openly about them let alone have an opposing view. One of the most obvious current area of disillusionment for some believers is scriptures discussion of homosexuality, in which the general interpretation is that God deems it sin (Leviticus 18:22). A subsection of Christians find it hard to reconcile the 'loving God' concept with the apparent rejection of homosexual people.

The equality of women, and in particular in leadership is also another debate that continues to fuel disillusionment for some (1 Timothy 2:11-12). Particularly with the presence of many successful businesswomen in secular work, the once readily accepted notion that women were unable to lead, are now not as culturally convincing. This has been the catalyst for some disillusionment especially amongst young women.

The doctrine of healing, which suggests that all sickness is not of God, has provided a lucrative environment for disillusionment to breed. Many believers have seen and lost loved ones and God's healing power has been absent. The inability to reconcile how a healing God, failing to heal someone they cared for creates a very painful loose end.

Institutions

In general, this generation is fairly anti-institution and anti-big business or corporations. They have developed good reason to distrust institutions, even though there are some organisations that are given almost infallible status, like Apple. They are very aware of large organisations and their greed, with little apparent social conscience like the current debacle involving Rio Tinto and its destruction of Juukan Gorge, the indigenous cultural heritage site. And after the global financial crisis in 2007, they are especially conscious of the risks of power and powerful people. For those young believers who find it hard to be in churches it's often because they are suspicious of the institution-like appearance that they believe resembles the inauthenticity of big business. It's the power-driven, no holds barred attitude to people and their communities that is a catalyst for disillusionment.

Injustice

This is possibly the most significant area of disillusionment, and certainly crosses over other areas mentioned above. Chapter 6 will further explore the significant injustices of prejudice and poverty.

Justice has an underlying belief that fairness governs the universe. And our tendency to see ourselves in a positive light means that we perceive ourselves as generally good, and label any behaviours directed against us as 'unfair'. Therefore, it doesn't seem fair when people prosper who have done bad things. It messes with our perception of a fair equitable universe. It's not fair when people who have hurt us, seem to bear no consequence for their actions.

It's important to know that this feeling is a common theme in the Bible. David remarks "Lord, how long will the wicked triumph?" (NKJV) in Psalm 94:3. Job says, "why do the wicked live and become old, yes, become mighty in power?" (21:7) And so can take some solace in the fact that this is not a new struggle.

As we progress through this concept, the hope is that you find some tools to consider this recurring question of injustice.

At this point, my agenda is simply to table these areas of disillusionment, and therefore begin to give readers some clarity towards healing.

In the next chapter we will begin to take a deeper investigation of the typical signs and language often present with disillusionment. We will consider the common reactions to disillusionment, and being to discuss the best postures for attaining healing.

King Solomon

Many people don't like Ecclesiastes, because it's clear that Solomon is in some kind of crisis. As far as we know, Solomon has pursued wisdom for most of his life. He was named the wisest person in the world, and was hailed for his wisdom across the globe. But in Ecclesiastes, Solomon sounds like a madman. At this point, he is in old age and is reflecting on all that he has done and assessing its worthiness. He explains that he has pursued success, beauty, pleasure and wisdom but alas he deems them "meaningless". The use of the word meaningless, *'hebel'* in the Hebrew, is unlikely to be suggesting the absence of meaning but rather highlighting the transitory and perishable nature of the things of this world.

WHAT ARE THE SIGNS OF DISILLUSIONMENT?

There are a few statements that King Solomon makes that give us some indication that he too may have come face to face with disillusionment. Firstly, he makes this comment:

> *"The wise have eyes in their heads, while the fool walks in the darkness; but I came to realise that the same fate overtakes them both. The fate of the fool will*

overtake me also. What then do I gain being wise?"
Ecclesiastes 2:14-15

After all his dedication to wisdom, Solomon faces this strange anomaly. None of his actions, often influenced by wisdom, gave him advantage over the fool. They both pass away. So essentially what was the point of it all? Did it really matter that he was wise? What was the benefit of his wisdom?

He then makes this statement:

> *"So, I hated life, because the work that is done under the sun was grievous to me."* Ecclesiastes 2:17

Another version says that it *"brought sorrow to me"*. This is certainly a depressing state of affairs.

Again, in verse 20:

> *"So, my heart began to despair."*

He even goes on to say that it is better for a person to never have been born (Ecclesiastes 4).

1 Kings 11 tells us that Solomon's eventual demise occurs at the hands of his wayward wives. Yes, he turns from God. I have read articles that have tried to say that it was the sin that caused him to turn away from God. Probably. But how could the wisest man in the world fall into the very temptation he so frequently warned others about? I'm not sure...but I certainly wonder if Solomon was disillusioned by all his meaningless pursuits and that was the first door that led him through to consider sin a good option. Because like Solomon said, *"what's the point?"*

King David makes a similar remark as his son, in Psalm 73:13

"Surely in vain I have kept my heart pure and have washed my hands in innocence."

David is also wondering how doing the right thing has benefited him. This is a big question common to the disillusioned.

WHAT CAN WE LEARN FROM SOLOMON?

1. You aren't alone

You are definitely not the first person to feel this way, and you won't be the last. Solomon knows how you feel. God is well aware of how you feel, and He has ministered through the generations to people just like you. He understands and He knows how to lead you out of it. You are not alone in your experience. Some may need to isolate for the purpose of processing, but you don't need to isolate because you are alone in your experience.

2. Even the wisest guy on earth struggled with disillusionment

Maybe you've felt like it's a slight on your existence to struggle with disillusionment. But just remember that Solomon in all his wisdom, was disillusioned too. Resist the urge to feel shame because of this. Shame is not a feeling produced by God. These are from the enemy's toolkit. There is no condemnation in Christ for what you are going through:

> *"Therefore, there is now no condemnation for those who are in Christ Jesus"* Romans 8:1

3. Stay away from sin

It's important to recognise that the temptation to throw it all in, and to follow your sinful desires is going to be high. Really high actually. It's hard to know what happens to Solomon's state of mind after Ecclesiastes, because the narrative goes silent. From the crisis we read about in Ecclesiastes it continues to his faith falling away and then death; see 1 Kings 11. But it's safe to say that Solomon probably didn't have a clear vision for where his crisis would lead. That is where we have an opportunity that Solomon didn't. One of the biggest factors that have helped me get through disillusionment, was the knowledge that God had more ministry left for me. I would eventually lead again and write. Neither of those trajectories would have benefited from an unhealed heart. So, in my prayers I would frequently ask God to heal me so well that there was never any evidence that I was ever even hurt in the first place. The healing process would be so successful that there would never be any reason for another person to question if I had ever been disillusioned.

This vision was my motivator. And surely this is the reason God puts dreams in our heart. It's not just because it's fun and inspiring. It's because when things get tough, we have something to walk toward. Because we might have to walk through the valley of the shadow of death, but that walk doesn't have to be directionless. So, what is it for you? What is your vision? Maybe you've never had an overall vision. Maybe God doesn't speak to you that way. That's ok. Just ask Him for one. And ask other people to pray that God would give you a vision. If you don't get it that is totally okay too. God may want you to use your reflection skills, so ask yourself where you want to be after all of this? If your vision is significant enough it will keep you from sin. It will keep you walking through the valley, even though it's hard. Because you know there is joy ahead.

4.   Faithfulness is the point

Solomon says this rattling statement:

> *"I have observed something else under the sun. The fastest runner doesn't always win the race, and the*

strongest warrior doesn't always win the battle."
Ecclesiastes 9:11

Prior to this, Solomon had it all worked out. The wise prosper and the fool leads himself to trouble. But then he realises this strange reality, that people don't necessarily get what they deserve. Sometimes people who don't necessarily deserve the reward, get what they want. Just like Solomon we want to believe that the effort and sacrifices we make throughout life will eventuate, to an outcome that we desired. But the reality is that not all of us will arrive at the place we desire to be. Despite all the sacrifices, pain and persistence, there are no guarantees in life.

So what did Solomon gain by being wise? What was the point of David doing good? What can we conclude about these valiant men and the high risk of disillusionment? Because we see it everywhere: sometimes the wife or husband who submits or serves ends up with the broken marriage. Sometimes the hardest working person and most gifted leader, doesn't end up with the corner office. Sometimes the most nurturing and loving people don't become parents. There are no guarantees in life. One plus one doesn't necessarily equal two.

See, Solomon doesn't appear to clearly answer his own question. Anytime he got right into the intricacies of this conundrum, he would throw his hands up declaring *"Eat and drink and be glad"* Ecclesiastes 8:15. But can you say that you are satisfied with that answer? I'm not.

In all my searches of the wisdom literature in the Bible (Job, Ecclesiastes and Proverbs) there is one word that frequently appears. One seemingly insignificant word:

Better.

It's better to live simply...it's better to be kind...it's better to have little...The only answer Solomon gives us for pursuing wisdom, is because it's...better. The reason we do good is because it is...better. It's better to do the things that God suggests are profitable, than to do the things that aren't. Because overall they may contribute to a better, more peaceful, joyful, or abundant life experience. There's certainly more likelihood of peace, joy and abundance when you do the right thing versus the wrong thing. The point is, if you are going to live, you might as well live better. It's an answer, but it's not an entirely inspiring one. After all, as Christians should we be satisfied with simply better? Don't we want what is best? I'm glad you asked! Just like Solomon, Paul also mentions a metaphorical race, that he reflects on as he approaches death.

> *"I have fought the good fight, I have finished the race,*
> *and I have remained faithful."* 2 Timothy 4:7

The greatest reason to pursue wisdom and goodness is because one day we will hear our Father in heaven say: *"Well done good and faithful servant"* Matthew 25:21. No matter what happens to you, if you have done your best to love and serve, you can be sure that you will hear these approving words. In the face of an unjust concept that Solomon presents to us,(that the fastest person doesn't win the race), Paul takes a different life changing perspective on the race of faith:

> *"Do you not know that in a race all the runners run,*
> *but only one gets the prize? Run in such a way as to get*
> *the prize"* 1 Corinthians 9:24

The faith race is not a competition. We aren't trying to beat other people to win. But if you carefully read the words in this verse, you'll notice that Paul's goal in this statement is not that we actually win the prize. He's not concerned with whether we win or not. He encourages us to run in a way like we will win the prize. The running is the focal point, and the quality of that run. This statement has never been founded on whether you arrived at the destination you had hoped for, it is founded on whether you were faithful in running.

Faithfulness has always been the goal of the race. Faithfulness is what gives your arduous journey meaning. Anything done in faithfulness is not a waste, and it is not pointless. It is the primary factor to which Jesus will remark when we finally see him in heaven. And when you hear these words every hardship you faced will dissipate in the presence of our pleased Saviour. This is the point. This is what we gain.

> *"Well done, good and faithful servant"* Matthew 25:23

CHAPTER 2

What does it look like in action?

It's not obvious to everyone, but it is possible for an Indian person to identify the specific region that another Indian person is from. I can generally tell if someone is from India or Fiji, and most Indian people can tell that my ancestors were from the South of India. There are specific qualities that as Indians, we intuitively identify when we are speaking to each other that give it away. It probably begins with language, as in dialect, but also specific terms that are common to people of each region. And of course there is the accent. But sometimes it can also be the physical attributes, like apparently my curly hair is a dead give away for my South Indian background. Whilst caucasian people might mistake me for South American, Egyptian, Lebanese or a range of other nationalities, to my Indian peeps they don't even have to work it out.

Whether we realise it or not, we pick up a lot from other people's language, appearance and behaviour. We decide whether we are going to trust someone based on their mannerisms. We invite people into our world because of the signs that they may be a worthy companion. We judge a lot of what we think on signs and language. Unfortunately, we don't always apply that same process to ourselves. The Bible tells us *"out of the abundance of the heart the mouth speaks"* Luke 6:45 . Which tells us that overwhelmingly, the core of our behaviour and language begins in the heart. Therefore to understand the inner workings of the heart, it pays to listen to what we say and what we do. The following are my top 10 signs of disillusionment and the top 6 statements of the disillusioned.

TOP 10 SIGNS OF DISILLUSIONMENT

1. **Shock**

   Shock can often feel like time has frozen still and you are hearing everything in slow motion. It is overwhelming and confusing. It's the emotional equivalent of being stung by a jellyfish. Whilst you are simultaneously realising that something isn't right, you are too confused to focus and figure it out. Shock is so common in disillusionment, because often it is precipitated by an event or occurrence. Shock can be very severe and you should consider psychological treatment if you are experiencing frequent and persistent flashbacks of a shock producing event.

2. **Confusion**

   Genuine confusion around the details of a situation, including difficulty to determine what took place, and why and how you arrived there, are very significant signs of disillusionment. When you are disillusioned, everything you once knew, now appears obsolete. Job makes an interesting comment.

   "Can people even speak when they are confused?"
   Job 37:20

   When you are disillusioned it can be difficult to articulate how it is affecting you. I imagine it is like clearing away the debris of a city that has just been destroyed. In that place of catastrophe and destruction, it's almost impossible to just start cleaning because you are still trying to comprehend the devastation.

3. Suspicion/Mistrust

Until foundations are safely re-established a person may find it hard not to be suspicious of other people and circumstances around them. Because our foundations and worldview are what gives us safety, and until meaning is re-established there is a preset suspicion of anything or anyone that may pose a threat to the re-establishment process or anything that reminds of the situation that contributed to the destruction.

4. Avoidance/Denial

The person who is disillusioned may avoid people or places that remind them of the truths they are struggling to reconcile. This is largely because of the pain and/or the confusion. At some point, it gets easier to pretend that the disillusionment doesn't exist because the pain and confusion can become unbearable and the gap between our expectations and reality seem unmendable. In my own experience, after finishing my staff role at a local church I tried to attend, but the triggers for pain and confusion were so inescapable that I would often avoid returning for several weeks.

The primary purpose of this kind of choice is protection. You presume that you were deceived and the best thing you can do is prevent deception reoccurring. And the best prevention is elimination. This is an occupational health and safety principle. If you have a high-risk activity, the first question you are to ask yourself is: Can I eliminate this risk? As in, can you do something so that the risk doesn't even exist. So, it is a worthy option. In fact, there are definitely times in which completely avoiding a particular disillusioning stimulus is wisdom. So, avoidance can be a good option at least in the short term. Although not so much in the long term though. Long term avoidance can also be recognised under another name. Denial can become your best friend when you're disillusioned. But what can be a more unprofitable mindset than denial? It literally hides opportunities for growth, because it is intent on psychological preservation.

5. **Anger with or without judgement**

The previous belief systems we held were tried and tested. Which means they were reliable, and they made us feel safe. To be at a place where there appears to be some solid evidence that your belief system was incorrect, can translate to anger. This new thing has disrupted your safety, it is threatening your security. How dare this new thing steal so much from you?! Often because our disillusionment relates to ideals we held, we will target the individuals responsible for challenging our ideals. This is where judgement comes in. Disillusionment will cause you to judge those individuals for what they did, or said, because they showed us a different possibly more cynical truth that we probably didn't want to know about. They broke our ideals. Judgement is a tough one, because often we are justified in feeling the way we do. Maybe they genuinely and deliberately hurt you. Maybe they sinned badly and let down a lot of people. Maybe they brought something intended to be pure, into disrepute. That's the thing with judgement, it often is justified if we were to look at singular circumstances under a microscope. But judgement is not the path of righteousness.

6. Loss and Mourning

Depending on the circumstances, disillusionment may trigger feelings of loss. It's usually directed at something: a future that you had dreamed of but no longer able to actualise. It could be the loss of time. It could be the life you enjoyed. You may have lost friendships and community. Either way it hurts and may need to be mourned.

7. Fear

If a wife cheats on her husband, there is usually no way the other spouse can pretend that everything is okay. The husband will naturally be afraid and nervous any time the wife goes near that other person. Or any man for that matter. Maybe not for the rest of their lives, but certainly whilst trust is being rebuilt. This fear is designed to protect us. It's supposed to warn us that a potentially threatening situation is about to unravel. This is why fear tends to appear when you are disillusioned. It's trying to protect you. Because your sense of safety is insecure when your belief system is damaged and in a temporary holding pattern. Of course, long term sustained fear is no longer protecting you. It now becomes a hindrance.

8. Indecision and Doubt

The experience of having trusted and relied on a set of beliefs that have now proven to be wrong, is all too fresh in the initial stages of disillusionment. The consequence is that the person will often have doubts about a lot of factors in their life. They may find it really hard to make any concrete decisions, or they go back and forth on a decision. This is all part of the absence of safety that has occurred.

9.   Isolation

When a disillusioned person is finding it really difficult to articulate why they are feeling the way they are, it can be really difficult as a friend or family member to handle. Because it also threatens our sense of stability, when someone changes how they are behaving. Unfortunately, we often try to change the person. We badger them, and try to throw every scripture or message we have heard at them in an effort to fix them.

Naturally, the person may retreat and isolate. Because, in that moment, they are working out that they are either going to disappoint people while they are going through this trial… OR they are finding the efforts to fix them really unhelpful. Either way, somewhere along the line they can come to believe that nobody is going to understand anyway.

10.   Numbness and Depression

Depression is very often coupled with disillusionment. And numbness can be a sign of depression. It can be because you are in a situation that has not been of your own doing. It can be as a result of feeling completely disempowered and stuck without a foreseeable hope of change. When you are forced to keep going without hope the numbness disconnects you from more pain and future onslaught. It seems easier than actually facing the truth of how much this thing has devastated you. I've seen plenty of church-goers in this place. Church leaders are so busy trying to engage them, but their numbness is not easily resolved when it is rooted in a lack of hope.

As an overall observation, disillusionment makes people feel unsafe. Emotionally unsafe. Because if nothing is true, then nothing is stable. And when disillusionment is persistent, it can have you doubt the realism of anything you have ever believed in. For instance, when a believer becomes disillusioned with one part of scripture it can shed doubt on all scripture. Which is why vigorous theological debate is often not the answer. At its core, it's often not even the scripture itself that is causing the disillusionment. It's the awakening of a new truth in light of an existing conflicting truth. It's how we deal with loose ends that is the cause of the stress arising from disillusionment.

TOP 6 STATEMENTS OF THE DISILLUSIONED

These are the most common statements that may be made by the person who is disillusioned:

1. **"How could they do that?"**

    This statement emerges as a result of shock. It's probably one of the first signs that there is a disconnect between a person's ideal and their reality, that they are struggling to reconcile. It's not a statement made in judgement although it can be. But usually it is genuine disbelief.

2. **"I don't really know what I think anymore"**

    This is typical of the confusion they are experiencing, and the process of reforming their opinions. They genuinely have lost hope in their previous beliefs and are in a place of confusion. This statement tends to come out particularly when being asked for an opinion. It's sometimes said in sadness or in capitulation.

3. **"I can't believe I could have been so naïve or ignorant"**

    This is often rooted in the regret of having put trust in someone or something that appears to have been an unworthy investment. It is also a statement of disbelief and disappointment.

4. **"I just can't do that again"**

> This statement comes from the persistent fear that restricts them even imagining a possible future in the place they were.

5. **"I've seen something that can't be unseen"**

> We all see things that we wonder about from time to time. But when you've reached the point of genuine disillusionment and you know that you cannot keep going as is, this comment is typical of that stage. It is the moment that a person realises that they cannot overlook or forget what they've potentially discovered.

6. **"What was it all for? What was the point?"**

> We've talked about this in the story of Solomon. Basically this comes from the sense of the loss of time. Having realised that you've spent so much time and energy commiting to a belief that you now consider may be misdirected, there is a feeling of loss.
>
> If you have said any of these statements, or know someone who has, it may be a sign that they are struggling with disillusionment.

CROSSROADS

The analogy of a crossroad is not at all a new one. There are songs about it. There is poetry written about it. There are entire novels, in which the primary backdrop of the plot is a crossroad. The crossroad analogy is so common, because it is universal. The vast majority of us will at some point make a decision to be with someone, or not. We will decide whether to try or give up. Study or work. The basic premise of this analogy is that often we have only two options to choose from. Yes or

No. Stay or go. And sometimes this is genuinely true. But there is a flaw in the crossroad analogy. It may seem like, when you are standing at a junction and there is a left and right path, and that you essentially only have two directions to choose from. But it's not actually true. There may be at least two other options:

1. You can go back
2. You can stay where you are

While not necessarily good options, nevertheless, there are options. We generally don't consider these options, because in the journey of 'moving forward' they do not suffice. The first option is definitely not 'forward'. And the second option is definitely not 'moving'.

Interestingly, whilst we may not consider either option, we often are defaulting to them while thinking that we've moved on. Some of us keep going back and some of us aren't actually moving at all. We might have changed everything around us, it may even feel like we have moved forward and chosen left or right, but it doesn't mean that our heads and hearts have come along with us. Sometimes they remain stuck at the crossroads.

Whilst the various behaviours and language associated with disillusionment has been detailed, ultimately we all have one choice. Either we genuinely move forward. Or we don't. This is your moment. By making the better choice, be prepared to take your head and heart along the journey. Moving forward means that you won't keep running. It means that you won't simply look to an external contextual change to resolve your hurts and frustrations. It means that you will only be satisfied with a heart change.

Either you get stuck, or you get free. So how do you tell if you are stuck? The key question is does it keep affecting you? This is a tough question, because often people try to tell themselves that it doesn't. Mainly because they do feel free when they are far away from the source of your disillusionment. When you're disillusioned with marriage, living a single life again seems amazing! Here's the downside of that - it's not a genuine freedom. It's just an escape. As believers we are destined to live a life of genuine freedom from fear and unrest, and instead have peace and joy in every circumstance. When you are no longer at the source of your disillusionment, you might feel lighter again, but if you haven't fully dealt with your disillusionment it will come straight back as soon as you get close again. That doesn't necessarily mean physically close. It includes psychologically and emotionally close. A better sign of freedom is whether you feel peace, when you are close to the original source of your disillusionment. Can you talk to your ex-partner and have peace? Or does it drum up all the feelings of disillusionment again? Can you visit your old church and feel positive and supportive about it even after you leave? Can you meet that person on the street and not wish you had taken another pathway? If you still have 'triggers', there's probably a good chance that you are not free.

So before you proceed, please consider what choice you are going to make. Are you going to do whatever you can to be free of disillusionment? And are you ready for what that might mean? Or are you going to stay where you are? Nobody is going to know the answer to this except for you. But it's still important to make a choice and follow that through. In the next section, I am going to tell you about the posture that is necessary should you decide to pursue healing from your disillusionment.

POSTURED FOR HEALING

The fact is, that God wants every one of us to be healed of our disillusionment. But disillusionment unlike anything else, is usually worked through rather than miraculously healed. This is due to the fact that there are mindsets being addressed, rather than spirits being expelled.

It's not usually an instantaneous process, as much as I hope to be proven wrong about that.

Therefore, if we desire complete restoration and healing it is critical to position ourselves as best we can for God to minister in and through us.

1.   Humility

In our frustration, it is easy to draw strong conclusions about why or how we have arrived at the place we find ourselves. It's a part of our inherent design to seek meaning, remember? But there are times when it is wise to suspend our incessant need to draw a conclusion, and allow God to lead us to the truth He wants us to find. It's part of trusting Him, that we rely on His interpretation of events rather than our own. Sometimes it is out of pain that we are quick to declare:

"It's their fault..."
"Marriage is bad..."
"Churches use people..."

But if you really want to be healed, suspend your desire to draw such a concrete conclusion. I realise that what I am suggesting is really hard to do in practice. But it's the only way to find true freedom and a deeper faith. Proverbs 3:5-6 says *"Trust in the Lord with all your heart and **lean not on your own understanding**; in all your ways submit to him, and he will make your paths straight."* This verse is quoted a lot. Because we know we must trust God with the various matters that face us. But it also means choosing to rely on Him for our interpretation of a situation. Humility is recognising that God knows infinitely more than the singular perspective that we are able to see through right now. With this posture, we are sufficiently stationed for healing.

2.   **Prayer**

Honest prayers are necessary when you are fighting against disillusionment. Prayer is one of the most powerful weapons we have in any stage of life. Sometimes when I say the word 'prayer' I feel like it can depersonalise what you are actually doing. When I say prayer, I mean the ability to talk to God as you would your best friend. It can be hard to do sometimes, because we are often told to revere God in a way that elevates His holiness but diminishes His personability. I'm not talking about disrespecting Him. I'm simply talking about being in constant communication with Him about where you are at, and asking Him questions that you expect Him to answer (even if those answers don't come immediately). Even when you feel like He is at fault for your predicament, you must keep talking to Him. Don't worry about what you say, speak from the heart as disagreeable as it sounds. He knows what you're thinking anyway. Sometimes He wants you to talk simply for your own sake.

3.   **Be ready for pain and ready for victory**

There is so much research out there about resilience. And I am certainly not even close to being any kind of expert on the matter. All I want to say here is that I think sometimes the most resilient people in life recognise that the challenges we face are only ever for a season. Yes, sometimes those seasons are longer than we think we can handle. But the resilient believer has a long term vision for victory through those challenges.

4.   Recognition

Be willing to recognise and call out the emotions that are going on inside of you. It took me a long time to realise that my apprehension about serving in a church again, was actually relating to fear At the time, I kept telling myself it was because my values and theirs were just too different and that "all churches are the same" or whatever rhetoric I used to cover up the real emotion that sat underneath the surface. But when I really knuckled down and asked God He shed light on the fears that I had been harbouring. It doesn't mean that the fear wasn't legitimate. I had good reason to be afraid! It hurt. But fear is not from God. Fear is not a helpful lens to see the world through. And my fears were completely misplaced. This was a different group of people who had shown me nothing but love and kindness. It wasn't fair for me to project my past onto them.

During the process of unhinging disillusionment, especially if you want to walk away completely free of its clutches, you will be tempted to project a lot of emotion on other sources. You will be tempted to blame. You will be tempted to cast judgement and even slander those who hurt you. Recognise what the emotion really is, and address those feelings with God. There's a good chance the reason you are being judgemental is because you are angry. Call it anger. Don't let it be hidden behind a more temperate name. You can't deal with what you can't see. You could be blaming others, because deep down you feel guilty or ashamed about something. Recognise what it really is, and call it out. It doesn't feel great sometimes, but it is definitely a better contributor to your healing than telling yourself that you are fine.

5. **Stay in some kind of relationship with other Christians**

For those of you with church disillusionment, I know that to suggest attending a church is just an impossibility for where you are at right now. BUT, it is still important to maintain Christian friendships during the healing process. Find people you trust, who aren't necessarily in the same place as you - unless they are also wholly committed to healing together with you. Find people who are understanding, who aren't going to judge you as you process your pain. The last thing you need is people around you who force you to filter your comments. It's okay if they challenge you, as long as it's not condemning. Make it a priority to catch up with those people regularly and ask them to be praying for you. If you don't have these kinds of friends, find them.

6. **Don't hold back the tears or the emotion**

We have a funny habit in the Western World. We think we are doing others a favour when we hold back our tears or painful emotions. The first time I went to a Western funeral, I was a little weirded out. Why were people not crying? I discovered that they were, but they simply dabbed their tears in an effort to hide their grief. My experience at funerals prior to this was exclusively Indian. People wail and cry openly. They may turn up with elegant clothes and a face full of makeup, but they don't let that deter the mourning process.

Now here's the thing. My own personal observations are that it seems like the people who let it out seem to mourn better in the long term. If you are still in the early stages of disillusionment, you may be hurting. My advice to you is LET IT OUT. Please don't hold back. Some emotional pain must be cried through. Yeah, you are going to get sick of it. But let the healing process take its course. When we cut ourselves, there is absolutely nothing we can do to rush the process. All you can do is facilitate good healing or make it worse. You can apply ointment, you can put on a band-aid. But you cannot do anything to make it heal faster than it's prescribed healing time. We understand this when it comes to our physical healing, but we are more impatient when it comes to emotional healing. And this is to our detriment.

I hope that if you have come this far through the book, that you are ready to start grappling with your disillusionment and find freedom. In the next chapter, we start to reconsider the purpose of disillusionment and how God can use it to make our faith deeper and more sustainable.

The Israelites and Egypt

The Israelites were the chosen people of God. They had incredible promise as a default of being in Abraham's bloodline. But strangely they found themselves slaves to a cruel ruler.

I'm talking about the classic story where Moses leads the Israelite people out of four hundred years of slavery to Egyptian rulers. The Israelite people were oppressed by the rulership of the Egyptians and they had called out to God, possibly with little faith that He would deliver. But God heard and he sent Moses to execute his plot, that included plagues, to lead them to their freedom. After finally being released by the Pharaoh, the Israelites' journey was to lead them to the promised land, a land flowing with milk and honey. Only, the Israelite people wandered in the desert for 40 years.

WHAT ARE THE SIGNS OF DISILLUSIONMENT?

In their time in the desert, the Israelites lamented often about their situation. In that place of discomfort they would express their longing to return to Egypt. Their lamentations often circled around the meat they ate back in Egypt (Exodus 16:3) compared to the provisions they had in the wilderness.

But Egypt was an illusion. It's so strange to think of a place of oppression, as a place of illusion. But they had become comfortable there. Most of them had not known any other way. Initially when the Israelites heard that God saw their struggles and was going to do something about it, they worshipped Him (Exodus 4:30-31). But later as they began to feel the consequences of Moses and Aaron's repeated enquiries of Pharaoh, they condemned them. They weren't willing to change their current situation if it meant it would upset the delicate equilibrium they had made with their Egyptian rulers. After 400 years of slavery, they had established and accepted the life they had, even though they were still slaves. They still had some joys and pleasures: an abundance of choice meats, a degree of peace with their rulers, and shelter. Often that is what an illusion is like. There is a measure of goodness to it. But it is a far cry from true freedom, and a real relationship with God. And just like we do, the Israelites became trapped in that place of wandering. They wandered for 40 years! They were unable to move forward as long as they continued to have the mirage of Egypt. Their stubbornness and misguided illusory worship of Egypt were the most significant signs of disillusionment.

WHAT CAN WE LEARN FROM THE STORY OF THE ISRAELITES?

1.   The Israelites had to fight for freedom.

When Moses and Aaron approached Pharoah, they did not actually request the once-for-all freedom of the Israelites. They only asked to be given leave for three days to venture into the desert and worship God. God's intention was for the people of God to be free forever from Egyptian rule, but He knew that the Pharaoh would have punished them severely for such a request, AND ultimately they wouldn't have been granted it. So all this time, as the many plagues released havoc, their request never changed: three days to worship God. But the Israelite overseers response after Moses and Aaron's first enquiry when the pressure first began turning up on account of Pharaoh's anger, was as though they were surprised that there might be some consequences to them for this request. This was such an unrealistic expectation. Pharaoh had been receiving free labour for 400 years. Why would he not put up a fight for this?? Every situation that I have ever heard, read or experienced myself where freedom is being pursued, has involved some kind of battle. Even when it's just to experience freedom in the heart. There has sometimes been an immediate cost and even a long term cost for freedom to be won. True freedom is like this. Because it usually affects someone or something, when the status quo is unhinged. If we want genuine freedom, as Jesus has desired to give, we must expect resistance. Whether it be from some external body, or even from our own flesh. It is a necessary reality. And it is what makes our freedom so beautiful; because we will never forget what it took to obtain it.

2. You will long for the illusion some days.

There are definitely some days that you, just like the Israelites, will wish for the past. When you were ignorant of the illusion, and you enjoyed it. There will be days when you will downplay the illusion, because it seems easier than where you are now. I certainly had some days when I lamented over having to see the truth, and wished that I could still do and be as I was. You actually convince yourself it was better. Even though you know you can't turn away from what you now know.

But in all your reminiscing don't let this truth evade you; your illusion enslaved you. Whatever your illusion was, you were serving it, probably not with joy and freedom, but with control and oppression. It may not have felt like that at the time, but it's the truth. Maybe your illusion was that you could have a perfect family. I'm sure it was a wholesome desire in response to the subpar family life you may have experienced as a child. This vision is not terrible. But without even realising it, this dream became your master. What if those in your family didn't want that? What if they wanted something different? Did you ask them what they wanted? Is it possible that you pushed some of them away, in your zeal? I've seen it time and again, to a degree in my own family. In my zeal to have had the family that I believed I missed, I forced my family members to live a life they didn't want and therefore created distance between us. The illusion did not improve my life over the long term. You may feel more vulnerable today, but you were actually more vulnerable in the illusion.

3.   The Promised Land is real, but needs redefinition.

Sometimes when I have heard the Promised Land talked about, I get this impression that we see it as a fantasy...#livingthedream. The image we get is of the Israelites being rich and living a life of luxury, pleasure and success. I'm sure we are likely appropriating it to our modern interpretation of the dream life. But the Promised Land was most significant to the Israelites because it represented a home. A place where they could be safe, that they could defend, where they could establish their own identity and their own culture and laws. They would no longer be foreigners in a land that conflicted with their values and held little respect for their divine calling. It's not something that the average person thinks about often, but the relationship between home and identity is huge. There is a significant impact on those who have been forcibly displaced from their homes. It's unsettling and insecure to experience such a situation, and often there are long standing psychological impacts. In the case of the Israelites their racial distinction also determined your level of freedom. Israelite in Egypt = Oppression. There was no sidestepping this, you were born into slavery.

Their Promised Land was referred to often as the land of milk and honey, which spoke to the fact that there would be provision and supply allowing them to cease their hard labour and striving. This description implied that it was a place of rest. Israelite in the Promised Land = Freedom and Rest. Rest didn't mean a place of inactivity and no work.

And it also didn't mean it would be like living in a resort or the things we define as 'rest', that are probably more associated with relaxation. It was a place of provision, not pleasure. The point I am trying to make is that, where God intends for us to be led when we come out of our illusions is a place of rest where we are no longer oppressed by rules and expectations. It is a place of ministering to the soul. Why is it that not a single modern development that surrounds me, can make me feel even a margin of peace and serenity than when I visualise the scene in Psalm 23? Because Psalm 23 so beautifully communicates the rest that is found under the divine hand of God. If God is dealing with an illusion, you can be assured that His intention is to move you toward a greater sense of inward restfulness. It's the kind of rest that labours out of worship, and not out of striving and inadequacy. And surely this is so much better than anything else we could possibly have in life. Is not the entire world ultimately trying to seek this? It's an incredible feeling, and I know that I am grateful now for the challenges I went through to be able to feel like this. There is probably no better reason to persist through your disillusionment than the inner rest you will enjoy at the end of it.

CHAPTER 3

Could there be a purpose to this?

Those of you who were around in the 80's may remember that awful black and white fuzzy stuff that appeared on your television screen when your aerial was broken. That black and white stuff was SOOO annoying, because it usually happened exactly when you had planned to watch your favourite weekly television program. It's not like now with Netflix or Stan, where you have the option of multiple devices and televisions. You usually had one TV, and if it wasn't working you were out of options. These days, if your connection is weak, you can always watch it at a later stage. Because all the episodes are there and they usually stick around for about a year or more (for many of us, this isn't a real problem because we've usually binge watched it the first week it came out and have to wait a whole year till we binge watch the next season). Back then, there was a real chance that you might just completely miss your favourite program. Not only was the fuzzy stuff so incredibly disruptive, it was also excessively noisy. And when it happened, every family member was on high alert trying to work out how to fix this thing. Sometimes, you would have a family member standing in the most awkward monstrous tree-like positions because that was the best spot to hold the aerial and get some kind of picture. And nobody laughed at these odd postures, we were all grateful that someone was willing to make the sacrifice to get back to the program. Because that was the main aim, to get back to the program.

There are a lot of disruptions in life, just like the black and white fuzz. They have the potential to get in the way of your plans, and unfortunately force you to rearrange the plans you made. Nobody would ever think that there was a purpose to the black and white fuzz, when you are trying to watch your program. Just like most don't assume that there is purpose to the distraction that took you off course.

During my seasons of disillusionment, I found myself frequently asking the question "How did I get here?" I had plans that didn't eventuate. There were goals that I believed I would have achieved before I hit 37 years old. I often looked back and felt like my future had been robbed. Maybe you can relate to this.

It can be really painful to be forced to redirect your life, when you never planned to. I used to see it every day in my role as a Rehabilitation Counsellor. People would come into my office after having a severe injury, and have to contemplate a completely new career path that they would never have considered had it not been for that one moment. Naturally some didn't deal with it very well.

It's hard for us to imagine that God may have had a purpose in our redirections. Once again, that doesn't mean He caused them. Certainly not so in the case of a broken marriage or a physical illness or injury. But sometimes the redirections are exactly what He planned. Like for myself. I was so focused on being a Pastor, that it would never have even occurred to me that God might have had another plan. And I deemed writing a 'disruption' for some time, until I was able to process my own disillusionment and see that this had indeed been His plan all along.

WHAT MIGHT BE GOD'S PURPOSE
FOR DISILLUSIONMENT?

God's ultimate purpose for disillusionment is (cue the epic drumroll)…
change. Sometimes in our circumstances. But almost always the change
pertains to our perspectives. I can hear you asking 'Why would we need
to go through so much just for a perspective change?' The answer is
somewhat in the question…if having to change our perspective can be
so painful why would we ever want to change them, except if we are
forced to? We like to think that we are really open to the transforming
power of God, but unfortunately we aren't always as open as we think.
Myself included.

Most of what we read in scripture should shock and astound us.
The scriptures are full of radical ideas. Counter-cultural ideas. Not just
for the world, but for Christian communities. Paul says he is content
whether he has FOOD or no FOOD. Food people. Food. I have never
even thought about the possibility of not being able to eat. The extent to
which my financial situation affects my eating habits, is whether I want
to upsize my meal deal. And most of us would be in similar situations.
Even those of us who have given up our careers in a full-time church
ministry role are generally well provided for in the Western world. And
yet Paul isn't even challenged by the fact that his sacrifice has left him
without food. This is radical thinking for our Western minds. We would
struggle without our smartphones, let alone meals. Actually some of us
would prefer to have no food, over no smartphone!

God wants to change us a lot. Not because we are unacceptable in
our design, but because we remain fundamentally flawed in our ability
to love and be selfless. All of this is to help us move toward a greater love
toward God and others (and even ourselves), in which God defines the
terms of love. This is the way in which God intends for us to impact this
world. Not necessarily with a lucrative career, or with accolades.

One of the most significant perspective changes I had to go through was a realigning of my understanding of Christian leadership. In general, I have very high expectations of leadership. Like many of us. For years, I honoured and respected those above me in leadership and believed that they were in their role because they were far superior to me in the leadership ability and character. I was willing to do far more than I probably should have sometimes, in service to their vision.

But then I came face to face with a hard truth. Christian leaders aren't perfect. In fact, sometimes they behave really badly. Deliberately so. It shouldn't be like that, but which of us can really judge. Power is not easy to handle. And neither is pressure. Put them together, and we all make choices that aren't wise. But when I was on the receiving end of some negative treatment, I fell into a pretty heavy disillusionment. Even months later, I found myself ruminating over memories that were preventing me from moving forward. I was unsure if I would ever be able to fully participate in a church again. I was definitely uncertain of whether I could ever serve or be a leader in a church again. Even though the Holy Spirit continued to affirm, through unusual means, that my future would bring me straight back to church ministry. I knew that I had to get through these memories and the disillusionment that were keeping me stuck, if I was going to be obedient to God in the future.

I undertook a process that I will introduce you to in this book, but in a nutshell I realised that I had been expecting Christian leaders to care for me and shepherd me. Actually, I just had a general expectation that Christians treat each other better. Now some of you are reading this and thinking that my expectations weren't unrealistic. And to a degree you are right. But when I really contemplated the ideas in scripture, I couldn't get past two truths. Firstly, Jesus calls himself THE GOOD SHEPHERD. There is nobody that is supposed to replace Him, in the love and care and leading that He gives directly to me. Every other Pastor and leader are co-shepherds. And that's only when they are choosing to be one. They are supposed to cooperate with Him in the care of the sheep. And sometimes they aren't perfect in that. Which should be fine with me, if I always turn to Jesus as my Good Shepherd. I had believed that they were supposed to be and do something for me, that only Jesus could do. In turn, I have been able to express a more selfless love to leaders in that I have forgiven them and extended grace. I also reserve my expectations for myself as a leader, instead of thoughtlessly assuming that they agreed to my terms. It's often the case with expectations that we rarely communicate them well to others, and rarely do we consult with the person in the process of developing those expectations...for them. This is an example of how God had been wanting me to change my perspective. He wanted me to be restored and realigned to put my trust in Him, rather than my trust in man. The purpose of this is not for you to critique my conclusions. It's simply a demonstration of the process of realignment and change that is intended in disillusionment.

So if God would have us change, what kind of changes would we expect to see?

Stronger Mentally and Emotionally

A few years ago, I faced one of the most intense times of anxiety and intimidation that I had ever faced. I was genuinely fearful of my future. When things began to really deteriorate, I caught on to what the enemy was doing. And I realised that I could not battle these things in the natural. I prayed constantly. I had scriptures that I reflected on throughout the day. I persisted through the situation, regardless of how I was feeling at the time. And as you can guess, the situation worked out in my favour. However, the best outcome of that season was recognising how strong I could be when I sincerely partnered with the Holy Spirit.

When I say stronger mentally, I don't at all mean being hard or obnoxious. I mean being able to stay focused and endure in the midst of a storm. Endurance is talked about a lot in scripture. Often the New Testament writers weren't advising the early church with technical leadership strategies. Rather, they were encouraging them to endure. Have you ever thought what it might mean to really endure through a hard season? It takes incredible resilience and focus. And yet, it is probably the greatest display of strength a human can demonstrate. The fact that Jesus endured the cross, is simply insane.

Clearer on the truth, not the illusion.

Even in Christian community we can choose to adopt an illusion over reality. In fact, often we prefer it. The number of married couples that I have believed were the epitome of God's design for marriage, only to be told that their marriages had fallen apart are too many to count. And I don't judge, because I know marriage is hard and have experienced it within my own. But there is something in me that wants to see couples like that. There is a desire in me to want to elevate these couples to a platform, that they didn't ask to be on. We hear them say that marriage is hard, but what we really hear is "people as amazing as us wouldn't struggle as much as you do." And it's not their fault. We want the illusion! Nobody wants to know that the things that happen in marriage can test you beyond what you are capable of. Nobody wants to know that sometimes you might wish that you never got married. Nobody wants to know that you can feel your loneliest when you are lying right next to the person of your dreams. We like the illusion, because it's rooted in a fantasy that we are valiant to protect.

I imagine that at times, disillusionment is the only way those bubbles can be burst because we do hold tightly to our fantasies. Fantasy is a self-serving world. Don't get me wrong, there are times when we have visions for a life that is of benefit to others. But fantasy is not vision. It's a place we escape to where we are often getting all that we want, exactly when we want it. In real life there's no way you will sustain a marriage if the sole purpose is to meet your needs. So, if you have any intention of enduring for the long term, illusions must be challenged. God's desired outcome of the disillusionment process is for you to walk away with truer conclusions about life and His plan for the earth, and not continue to affirm the illusion that has often stood between you and what God really wants to do in and through you.

More surrendered

You could argue that the trajectory for every follower of Jesus is a steady path toward a greater depth in your relationship with God, and an increasingly surrendered life to Him. See, if you journey with God for long enough, you will find that you are in a fairly constant cycle of giving up and laying down. It is the process of taking up our cross. We don't necessarily take it up all at once. Our selfishness and self-focus limits our capacity to carry that cross all at once, without breaking our metaphorical backs. But Jesus knows that, and hence why He is patient. Selfishness and self-focus are the greatest items of agenda on God's plan of transformation. And if He can use disillusionment to help us move toward selflessness, He will.

Softer heart and humility

If we come out of our disillusionment, we are crowned with the most radiant of all postures; we become humble. There was a time when I used to judge the people who walked away from church. Now I look at them with compassion and understanding. Not because I accept their choice, but because I have a greater awareness of how hard it is to stay connected in a community of believers when you feel vulnerable to further hurt, pain and confusion. Going through disillusionment can give you a softer heart. Having a soft heart makes you more ready to serve and love others. It makes you more willing to take a chance and reach out. The amount of times I have yelled out to God "SEND ME!" since He has healed my disillusionment is too many to number. THIS is what a soft heart does. It reorients you.

Greater direct revelation and intimacy

When we are in the early phases of our relationship with God, we can become reliant on our Pastors to feed us. We come to services every Sunday needing to hear their word to make it from one Sunday to the next. This is not ever where God wants us to stay though. At some point, a child no longer relies on a parent to deliver food into their mouth. There is nothing quite so powerful as direct revelation. If we are only ever hearing someone else's revelation, we miss an opportunity to hear for ourselves what God desires to express only to us.

For myself, I have had such an increase in my ability to hear how the Holy Spirit wants to lead and guide me. He intends for you to be able to hear his voice and discern his leading for yourself. This is only achieved through a growing intimate relationship, which can be hindered by your illusions.

Discernment and wisdom over absolutes

Sometimes we think it is faith, but we tend to have a lot of rigid statements as believers. For instance, we assume it's not being faithful to give something up, when the reality is that it could be an act of surrender. Unfortunately, we tend to make

choices according to these statements without really quali-
fying them. An example might be that you must read your
Bible everyday, for an hour, in the morning. Sure these are all
things that are beneficial, but they certainly aren't mandatory.
For some this can be an overbearing burden to accomplish.
We unknowingly can give such statements a law-like superi-
ority that determines how righteous we feel. After journeying
through disillusionment, my understanding of walking by the
Spirit has exponentially grown. I wasn't supposed to put my
faith in these overarching rigid statements, I was supposed to
rely on the Spirit to help me discern the tools needed in any
given situation. This is obviously not the case with sin. An
example of the difference discernment makes might be, our
choices for entertainment. One person might watch a television show and be confronted with all sorts of temptations to
consume alcohol or seek out lustful experiences. Another person might watch a show and find that it has no effect on their
faith. Discernment is what helps a person determine which
programs are best to stay away from, on account of the individual differences in temptation. See, black and white rules
(again the exception being sin) are only made where people
can't be trusted to be wise. But we have all been given the
Holy Spirit and God wants us to rely on the Spirit to determine His specific path for us. Because the Holy Spirit knows
us so well and knows what is good for us. As you grow in your
relationship with God and are able to understand more of
how the Holy Spirit uniquely speaks to you, it is wise to turn
to the Holy Spirit to know how to walk than to put your trust
in statements that may not be true in every situation (again
the exception here is sin).

THE ENEMY'S PLAN

As believers, I think we all too often overlook the agenda of the enemy in the trials we walk through. I don't believe it should be our focus, but we should acknowledge that he stands to gain from our reactions to the situations that are put before us. Disillusionment is a great distractor from this fact. Disillusionment in itself is not wrong. It's unpleasant. But it's not necessarily wrong. It has the potential to deepen our faith, if stewarded well. But when you are in the thick of it, and you are absorbed by the feelings therein, it's hard to acknowledge that spiritual beings beyond you are invested in how you weather this challenge. The enemy definitely has a plan and a desired outcome for your disillusionment including:

Intimidation

The enemy likes to make us think that we are powerless. It couldn't be furthest from the truth. The reality is that we are incredibly powerful, and that he has every reason to fear that which is in us on account of the Holy Spirit. But, that doesn't mean that he is not effective in averting us by his plans. When we face disillusionment, we become aware of how ill-equipped we are to deal with certain issues. We feel defenceless and powerless. This is the way in which the enemy intimidates us. When we are feeling vulnerable to attack AND we don't believe we have valid methods or equipment to rise up to that challenge, we feel intimidated. The real risk with intimidation is the fact that it can stop you from trying. It can stop you from trying again. It's a feeling that we don't enjoy and we will often do anything we can to not be in situations that intimidate us.

Hard-heartedness

Unprocessed disillusionment can make us very angry. It can make us cynical and bitter. However, the outcome of all negative emotions like these are its propensity to make us hard-hearted. I can't think of a single posture more detrimental to your relationship with God than hard-heartedness. It makes it virtually impenetrable for God or anyone else to reach those parts of your heart that are also responsible for the good you do. It limits the expression of love. It limits faith. It limits the fruits and activity of the Holy Spirit. We hear of hard-heartedness mentioned throughout scripture. The Pharaoh of Egypt took his people through untold pain on account of his hard-heartedness. Stiff necked and hard-hearted, is sometimes how God described the Israelite people. In the Old Testament, Zedekiah, rebelled against King Nebuchadnezzar and became hard-hearted and would not turn to the Lord (2 Chronicles 36:13) Inflexibility makes us unwilling to follow the leading of God. which is exactly where the enemy wants us. He makes us believe that He is on our side by luring us into this indifference, but the opposite is true. He is invested in our demise.

Give up

The ultimate outcome for the enemy is that we would give up. He knows that if he can get us to give up in certain areas of our faith journey, that the path toward getting a person to give up altogether on God is not that far off. It does often happen this way too. We wonder if God really cares. We wonder if He is genuinely good like we've been told. Our belief in God is decreased, when our vision of Him diminishes. And if the enemy can have us doubt who God really is, the vision starts to crumble.

Every one of these agendas are ultimately harmful to you. And yet, often when we are wading through disillusionment we are unable to recognise that there is an outcome intended by other parties. In fact, sometimes we aren't even really thinking about the probable outcome for ourselves.

REVELATION

The significant change that we must undergo, where necessary, is our approach to scripture. There is a reason we haven't seen the revelatory truths that would have broken through our illusions without these traumatic events. We aren't always looking for that deeper exposition of scripture that is necessary to find the gold within. To find real gold, companies erect massive drilling rigs to dig and dig until they find it. We aren't really supposed to just read scripture. We are supposed to be seeking God. The task of seeking God is not achieved by skimming over a few verses. To seek God is to engage every part of your heart to find the truth. Don't glaze over verses, giving them a mental nod. Pull them apart and force yourself to consider those parts that sit outside of your current level of understanding.

Sometimes in Christian society, the preaching of God's word has become not much more than an inspirational word that makes you feel good. Consequently, we are in the habit of seeking inspiration in scripture, not necessarily the truth. Inspiration doesn't necessarily change us. It affirms us. Sometimes we need affirmation. But inspiration is a rather shallow motivator. Revelation, on the other hand, is completely reliant on the activity of the Spirit of God and His choice to uncover the goodness that resides within Him and His Word. The agenda we bring to the scriptures will affect what we see in it. To really see the truth of God in your situation, you're going to have to go beyond your own preconceived understanding of faith and pursue the revealed truth that can only be found through prayer and reflection, grounded in the Word of God.

So what exactly is revelation?

Remember when you were a kid and you played pass the parcel at birthday parties? It was so much fun! You either got the big prize, or you get one step closer to revealing the big prize, or you have a chance of getting a rather insignificant gift on the journey to the big prize…or you get more wrapping paper…either way you got something!

This is much like the nature of God. He is an ever-unfolding prize and mystery. At every layer there is some kind of opportunity, only the gifts are never unimportant. They are always of great value.

I would never have considered myself a complacent believer. I read my bible every day, often spending over an hour in contemplation and prayer. I was at church every week. I went to conferences. I participated and led small groups. But when I look back on my time as a Pastor, I would say that there was a sense of complacency, despite doing and feeling like a typical passionate believer. When I say complacency, I guess I am referring to the lack of awe I had accepted in my image of God. I had essentially 'figured' out the nature of God. Or so I thought. I wasn't pursuing Him anymore. I saw my time with Him, as a time of filling up and equipping for my calling. But after I left ministry, and spent a few months just healing and resting, something began to change. I rediscovered the wonder of God. He is actually incredible. He encompasses divine attributes, with complete perfection. His love is literally mind blowing. His grace is absurd. And whilst I am focusing on my relationship with Him, there is a whole universe beyond me that He is sustaining. Have you ever thought about the earth and the solar system? Is it not a miracle that these planets are able to move and stay in a cyclic pattern for thousands of years, and yet never be drawn into the sun or each other? And what about the sun! It is ridiculously powerful, and yet beams the perfect amount of light across the galaxy to sustain all of earth's needs. It's simply remarkable! And this is our God, who perfectly orchestrates all. There is so much mystery to God. There are so many aspects of His being that we don't comprehend.

A most interesting fact about God, is that as much as we can seek and pursue Him, it is still up to Him to reveal Himself to us. And when He reveals Himself to us, it is almost always life changing and transformational. That's what happened all those years ago when I had my 'God is real' moment. He showed me a truth about Himself that I could not have found for myself. I could have recited "God is real" to myself for the next 20 years, but if He didn't reveal it to me it would never have moved me to the place of knowing.

For some, walking through this disillusionment, is going to require an overhaul to interacting with God's word. And it will start with acknowledging that you need God to reveal Himself to you, and reveal the truth that lies within scripture to tie off those loose ends. But here's the good news: God always wants to reveal Himself to us. The scriptures are basically one intricate tale of God's revelation of Himself to humankind. Both corporately and personally. God does not want to withhold Himself from us. But He is also, to a degree, selective in His timing in self-revelation. But God assures us that there are things we can do that move His heart to reveal more of Himself:

> *"Come near to God and He will come near to you"*
> James 4:8

> *"You will find me, when you seek me with all your heart"* Jeremiah 29:13

> *"Knock and the door shall be opened unto you"*
> Matthew 7:7

God is all too pleased to meet with the person who is resolute in finding Him.

In the next chapter, we begin to get practical in processing disillusionment. Some Christians don't really believe that emotions need to be processed. The reason I chose a word like 'processed', is because I believe that there are some ideas that must be broken down. Let me explain through a rather disgusting analogy (apologies in advance). When you put food in your mouth, it is first broken down by your saliva and the chewing process. Then it travels down to your stomach and through your intestines. Throughout this process, the body is continuing to break down the products consumed through enzymes and digestive functions, to extrapolate that which can be used to build your body and that which is to be discarded.

There is a classic Seinfeld episode that every fan can quote verbatim. Kramer and Jerry, two of the main characters, are invited to observe a surgical procedure being done on one of their friends. They are seated in a viewing gallery in which they can see the operation, at a safe distance. Kramer is clearly peckish and pulls out a box of Junior Mints. A small chocolate mint the size of a coin. Through a series of unfortunate and humorous events, a single mint flies up in the air and drops right at the entry point of the surgery, unbeknownst to the surgeons. The friend's health takes a turn for the worst, and nobody but Jerry and Kramer know why. They try to reason that people eat bucket loads of those Junior Mints, but obviously it goes through the digestive process. They aren't placed next to vital organs! Don't worry, the friend's health improves miraculously, and all ends well. But no one will ever know what became of the Junior Mint, and its impact on his recovery.

The fact is that disillusionment is much like the digestive process. It must be broken down, lest we remain confused and afraid. We must chew on it. We must give it the best chance of the goodness being digested, and the not so good being discarded. To do anything different with disillusionment, is equivalent to placing an object that doesn't belong near vital organs. We ultimately don't know what the long-term damage will be. But it certainly won't benefit us and it cannot nourish us in the wrong place.

Let us now proceed with the metaphorical digestive process…

Jeremiah

God gave Jeremiah the mammoth task of being a prophet to the Israelite people through a time in history, when very few were listening to the wisdom of God. God intended to bring judgement upon the Israelite people and Jeremiah was chosen to be a key messenger for all that would come. Jeremiah courageously declared the word of the Lord and faced many personal consequences for doing so. But the story of Jeremiah gives us expansive insight into the personal journey of a man that was so often rejected by those around him for the prophecy he shared.

WHAT ARE THE SIGNS OF DISILLUSIONMENT?

We can read in Jeremiah Chapter 11, that a plot to kill Jeremiah was revealed unless he ceased to prophecy. It's upon this realisation that Jeremiah appeals to God with this very raw conversation:

> *"You are always righteous, Lord, when I bring a case before you. Yet I would speak with you about your justice. Why does the way of the wicked prosper? Why do all the faithless live at ease? You have planted them, and they have taken root; they grow and bear fruit. You are always on their lips but from their hearts. Yet*

you know me, Lord, you see me and test my thoughts about you." Jeremiah 12:1-3

This is such an interesting cry out from Jeremiah. He is watching the wicked succeed and yet God is testing him? I'm sure you've felt this way. I have. It seems like the people who have hurt you, are unphased by their own sins. And God even seems to be blessing them. And yet God is pointing out your sin. And telling you to grow? Disillusionment certainly starts with such questions.

The response from God, in all honesty, comes across as rather dismissive:

"If you have raced with men on foot and they have worn you out, how can you compete with horses?" Jeremiah 12:5

Um, gee thanks God…It doesn't seem like the most encouraging comment, really. What we expect God to say is something like "Jeremiah you are a man of God. Don't get distracted, don't compare, just trust me. My justice is righteous and pure." Something along those lines that reassures. But He doesn't. So, what does this statement really mean?

God's agenda in this statement is to remind Jeremiah that there is more hardship to come. And it is true. God knows that Jeremiah is probably scared, and definitely discouraged by the threat. But there is still more that God has intended for Jeremiah, which should affirm that this recent threat will be of no ultimate effect to his overall life. Plus, the real threat is against the people of Israel.

Jeremiah continues to prophecy after this interaction with God as he had been. But by Chapter 20, Pashhur, the official in charge of the temple, had Jeremiah beaten and put in stocks. Jeremiah doesn't immediately respond with praise to this, in fact he turns back to God in

Jeremiah 20:7 and says, *"You deceived me, Lord, and I was deceived!"* This is probably the statement most indicative of disillusionment.

Jeremiah had believed that by his prophetic words he would be pulling down the enemies of the Israelite people. Instead, he is prophesying against his own people. Furthermore, he thought that he would be delivered from his enemies, and instead he has been physically beaten by them. This was not what he had imagined. But as he progresses conversationally with God, his response starts to change. He recognises that try though he might, he simply cannot contain the message God lays on His heart (Jeremiah 20:9). And he reassures himself in verse 11:

> *"But the Lord is with me like a mighty warrior;*
> *so my persecutors will stumble and not prevail."*

He still continues to lament painfully but he also declares God's Word to the Israelite people as harmful as it may be to his future safety and security.

He then arrives at Chapter 26 and again his life is threatened, now for a third time. But his response is completely different. He compels them again to reform their ways, but as for himself he says, *"do with me whatever you think is good and right"*. He is fearless! Their threats don't seem to even hit a nerve. Is it so far-fetched that he would be unafraid of such threats, when he has survived them twice before? Of course, he doesn't die here. He goes onto face even more trials. But he never stops speaking the Word of the Lord, despite the direct personal consequences for doing so.

WHAT CAN WE LEARN FROM JEREMIAH?

1. It's okay to bring your frustrations to God

Jeremiah didn't hesitate to lament to God about his circumstances. God did not see it as a lack of faith, nor did He withdraw His calling for Jeremiah's reaction. God is definitely fine with our emotions. Unfortunately, we are often not fine with our own emotions. There are a few reasons for this. Firstly, we can tend to be very judgemental of ourselves, and quick to label our responses. We can either judge ourselves as 'unfaithful' or 'negative'. And this is where we can run into problems. Yes, sometimes we do have negative and unfaithful thoughts. We aren't supposed to deny them, we are supposed to keep taking them to God. He has promised to accept us fully, and not just with the areas of our lives we think He likes. We can be completely honest as we express our feelings to God. It is more likely those feelings are changed as He responds to our prayers. We may not get the answer we want, and we may not even get an answer. Because sometimes the purpose of prayer is relational transformation.

2.   Recognise that disillusionment is not supposed to be the end

Whilst the story may have taken some time to unpack, this reflection on Jeremiah demonstrates the three stages that he went through to arrive at a place of fearlessness in his mission. We see a great example of someone who was able to travel through the challenges that disillusionment repeatedly threw at him.

Firstly, Jeremiah responds in obedience to God, even when God doesn't appear to respond to Jeremiah's cry. Then Jeremiah endures physical violence upon His life. And then He endures further intimidation. In all of Jeremiah's days, he never stopped prophesying what God put on his heart. That first disillusionment was not supposed to be the end, there was an incredibly lengthy story that was unfolding. If he had thrown his arms up at the supposed injustice of God at the first time it appeared, he would have never fulfilled all that he was destined to. Disillusionment is only ever supposed to be a destination that we pass through. It's often necessary for us to redefine our beliefs, so that we are equipped to deal with the rest of the journey.

3. God intends for us to run with horses

It was never the destiny of humankind to compete at the lowest level. This is what spiritual warfare is all about. The devil and his demonic forces are our real enemy, not man. It requires us to always be growing in our level of resilience if we ever expect to be all that God calls us to and contribute to the Kingdom the way God has intended us to. We aren't 'mere humans' anymore. Our natural default for living, is not the standard we were called to. We are humans with spiritual authority, and any challenge that is thrown at us is one that is fought in the spiritual realm. The Bible promises us that we can step on the serpent and scorpion. Jesus has delegated authority to us, to thwart the plans of the enemy. We are a restriction to him. A barrier to his evil plans. From each trial, challenge and disillusionment, we can be restored to a greater level of faith that transcends beyond the attacks the enemy used to throw at us in the past. We become conquerors, and we are able to run with the horses just as Jeremiah proved He could do.

CHAPTER 4

Digesting disillusionment

If we return to the ship and fog analogy back in Chapter One, we are reminded that there are a couple of significant factors that restrict the activity of an individual clouded by disillusionment:

- The fog skews visibility
- The fog skews audibility

As long as your senses are impaired you will probably not feel safe enough to move forward. And many believers don't. Sometimes God does want us to move forward, even when we can't feel, see or hear something that gives us confidence in the direction we should move. This part of the journey of trusting God is called faith. When I was working as a Pastor at my local church, and I started to sense the leading of the Holy Spirit toward writing, I was excited, but I was also hesitant. I had so many reasons to disqualify myself. I wasn't well known, I hadn't received my full pastors credentials, I had never written a book before… there wasn't a single reason visible to me to believe that anything I wrote would ever make a dent in the Christian world. And truthfully, I still don't know. And that has been my 'walking in faith' journey.

For you, your 'walking in faith' journey has probably been reading this book and starting and hopefully finishing a process of healing. You were probably unsure if you really wanted to read this, and you may have been unsure whether you ever really wanted to think about all this stuff again. I'm sure you have had lots of questions, doubts and even fears. My objective in this next section is to give you more clarity that should effectively begin the process of clearing the fog, enough for you to see and hear a way forward. If you haven't found some hope in the pages of this book already, this is where we will get downright practical about healing.

ONE PRAYER

Sometime in my 20's, I began a useful practice. I had gone through a season where I struggled to seek God. I didn't seem to have the motivation to read the Bible, and I prayed intermittently. I even stopped reading Christian books and listening to worship music. I just didn't have the desire to seek Him anymore, and whilst I had a good idea why, I had no idea how to fix it. After trying everything I could possibly think of, and continuing to add to my guilt, I had an epiphany. If I really believed that the *prayer of a righteous person is effective'* (James 5:16), then all I really need to do right now is pray for just one thing, consistently. So I began praying that God would give me a desire to seek Him. I prayed this one prayer everyday, and that is pretty much all I did. I didn't pick up a Bible unless I genuinely felt like it and I didn't pray unless I felt prompted to. What do you think happened? It took a couple of months, but I ended up with a love in my heart for God and His Word that drew me into a deeper relationship with Him. He changed my heart instead of me trying to change it myself. I have continued to practice this periodically throughout my adult life. I prayed for an increase of faith for six months, and I grew seriously in my faith. I prayed for an eternal perspective for a few months, and I found myself pursuing God in a totally different way.

See, we often have a tendency to over complicate matters. We panic and try to resolve our problems in our own strength. We make brash decisions and label ourselves because we feel the pressure of our emotions. But we often don't end up at the place we intended, despite all our activities. The alternative, is to just focus on the one thing that you think is central to your journey right now. Here's a hint, it's probably going to be something that is core to your relationship with God, rather than just some external factor. It could be peace in the midst of a storm. It could be patience with the church. It simply could be more love for Jesus. Whatever it is, choose wisely because it may take some time for this prayer to come to pass. And when it comes to pass, you want it to have the life changing quality that only God can produce.

CONSIDER YOUR ROLE

I want to preface this section by saying that there are many things you should not take responsibility for. If you have been in an abusive relationship, you do not have to take responsibility for your partner's choices. Full stop. And there are a multitude of other situations where this rule also applies. This doesn't mean that you can't reflect on whether there has been a part that you played in the disillusionment, NOT THE ABUSE. Just the disillusionment. You may have had illusions that are worth reflecting on. Maybe you believed that a spouse would complete you, and threw caution to the wind when you met your partner. You aren't responsible for what they did, but believing that a spouse would complete you is an illusion. And it's worth owning that, if firstly you want to heal, but secondly, if you want to ensure that you never end up in that situation again. You may have been a victim, but you don't have to keep wearing that label. You can be an overcomer. The possibility is the ability to be an overcomer whilst still having a victim mentality. It at least appears to be an oxymoron.

The whole point of recognising your part is to take responsibility for that which was actually your responsibility. As much as I would like to blame 'church' for the times I have come close to burnout, I made choices that had a significantly negative contribution to my health. There are times where I actually had the choice to say no to a task. Yes, I might have been unpopular for a time, but it was still my choice. I failed to consider my physical and mental health. But most of all, I cannot blame any other person for my aggressive status-oriented ambition, and the incessant desire to be a 'somebody', because I felt inadequate. That was entirely on me. Of course, it's a terrible combination to have that level of inadequacy and then work in a performance driven environment, but I still chose to make decisions that were driven by that voice in my head. And when I realised what I had been doing and the way it bated me into the situations I had often blamed church for, I repented. As justified as I felt, I repented because I would probably never progress in life or heal, as long as I refused to take responsibility for my part. I must take responsibility for my mistakes or illusions, if I ever want to make some kind of plan toward prevention. This is not to say that the church may need to repent for certain behaviours too, but I am ultimately not responsible for that. That is between church leaders and God. I have no right to judge whether they ever do that.

Here is another area that is worth bringing to the table for consideration now; have I been trusting in my ideals instead of God? I trusted and believed in ideals; the illusions that became 'dis-illusions'. Some of them may not have been true. Some of them may have been standing in the way of my relationship and service to God. I worshipped the idea of being successful in ministry, more than I worshipped God at times. I wanted to be this great Pastor, who would eventually run a 'successful' church. There was only one problem with that; it was all about me. I told myself that it was in service to God, but who was I kidding? It was all about me. It was a search for validation. Not just for myself, but with my peers. We all have our illusions that we believed, that under the surface were not as righteous as we imagined. Even the desire to find my 'ideal' church, was for my own pleasure and sense of rightness. Am I wrong for having wanted the church to be better? Not necessarily. But the illusion was that I wanted the church to be better because *I* thought it wasn't right. There was a measure of selfishness in my desires. And there again, is a demonstration of an illusion, with its measure of truth. The Church should always be growing and becoming better and more faithful than it was in the past. But not necessarily to meet my needs.

It is important to repent of all matters that might stand between you and God. This is an act of humility. Repenting doesn't mean that you have to stop being angry. Sometimes our anger is righteous. Repentance doesn't mean that the person who caused you pain is justified. It simply means that you offer your heart up to Him, and be open because Jesus is asking you to. In Matthew 7:3 it says:

> *"Why do you look at the speck of sawdust in your brother's eye and pay no attention to the plank in your own eye?"*

Whether you were right, or they were wrong, is not nearly as important as the state of your heart.

FORGIVE YOURSELF

When you realise that you have bought an illusion you can feel pretty discouraged. Shocked. Angry at yourself. You are not alone in this experience. A study completed by two scientists almost 10 years ago, shows a video capturing two teams passing a basketball to each other. The researchers asked the observers to count the number of passes made by one team, and they were asked to supply that number at the end of the video. They were then asked if they happened to see the gorilla that walked through the midground of the video. What? A gorilla? Yes. During the video, a woman dressed in a gorilla suit walks right in the middle of the visual and pounds her chest and walks off. Amazingly, only 50% of the observers saw the gorilla.

The researchers were intrigued by the response of those who missed the gorilla, which varied between shock and outright denial. In most cases, the person believed that they would have seen something so distinctively different in the midground. The researchers termed this phenomenon "the Illusion of Attention". We presume that we are more attentive than we actually are. We presume that we will see the gorilla, but we don't.

You need to forgive yourself. Because we are all susceptible to illusions. Mature Christians are no exception. It's not necessarily a reflection of wisdom or knowledge. We can all grow and improve our discernment of illusions, but that doesn't mean we will detect them all the time. Even as I write, I know that I probably have illusions that I am unaware of. And when God decides to show them to me, I will have to go through this process again too. So, go ahead and forgive yourself. You are no different to everyone else in this experience...we all accept illusions.

FORGIVE THE OTHER PERSON

There is a good chance that you may have to forgive some people in light of your disillusionment. Jesus talked a lot about forgiveness. He wanted to make sure that we knew that there is supposed to be no limit to the number of people, the number of times, and the size of the matter...when it comes to forgiveness. This is all based on the fact that we ourselves are undeserving of forgiveness, and God Himself forgives those who hurt us...therefore we have no right to withhold that which God freely gives. To withhold forgiveness is to suggest that we are also unworthy of forgiveness.

It is important to note that forgiving another person doesn't mean that their actions are now justified. It doesn't mean they deserve forgiveness. It doesn't mean that there aren't consequences to their actions. It doesn't mean that you don't legitimately need some distance from them. It doesn't mean you have to pretend that it doesn't still hurt. It is simply moving to a place where you are able to let go of the desire to see them earn the consequences of their actions. When someone hurts you, there is a mental and emotional exchange that occurs internally, like a loan account has been initiated. A large amount that they don't have has just been deducted. Internally, we now believe that the person is accountable to us for anything they do because they owe us. Imagine your flat mate complains that they can't pay the rent, but then they buy a big screen TV. They can't be buying a TV when they owe you rent? Right? It's the same with unforgiveness. Forgiveness is cancelling the debt. It's offering up to God the destiny and consequences of their choices. And leaving it to Him to rectify. It's trusting that you will be vindicated, without having to see negative repercussions come to the life of the person who hurt you.

As a society, people seem incredibly reluctant to reconcile and say sorry. Christians included. A genuine apology is really important to God. He expects us to reconcile with others, as He reconciled us to Him. The point is, there are a lot of believers having to process unforgiveness, without closure. It is really helpful relationally to have closure, and without having that person say, "I'm sorry, I did wrong against you" it is that much harder to move on. Unfortunately, the person who has been hurt has had to hear every preacher harp on about unforgiveness, meanwhile the person who has done the wrong has gone unaddressed, unrepentant and hardly even challenged. Or so we think.

As for you, the person who has been hurt, I want to say that you probably should have received an apology. And as much as I will stand up on my soapbox and encourage believers to take responsibility for their actions, I know that there will be many who will never heed my advice. Which means that you will have to continue forgiving without closure. But this is where I believe God will honour you. When you can forgive without the apology, God will honour you for your faithfulness to forgive.

RELEASE PEACE

Peace is a remarkable subject. Peace and joy have got to be the two most popular topics written about in the Christian social media world. So many of us feel like we either don't have it, or we could use a whole lot more.

How does peace align our frame of mind?

1. The origins of peace are through the Spirit.
2. This means that peace is a predominantly internal experience.
3. Peace is primarily received.
4. The peace of God can be limited by us, when we have conflicting beliefs.

As a society we will often look to external matters to resolve the inner conflict we feel. We look to a person to fix our loneliness. We look to our organisational skills to prevent feeling overwhelmed. We look to our bank balance to feel financially 'secure' or more accurately, to find 'financial peace'. Or we look to a new church to experience community. Being organised, having friends and having money aren't the enemy here, but we are often habitually prone to searching out external solutions to resolve our internal experiences.

Also peace is received. This is different to our assumptions, that usually presume that internal peace can be obtained in our own external efforts. Jesus stated, *"Peace I leave with you; my peace I give you"* (John 14:27). Jesus gives us His peace. It's not just any peace. It's the kind of peace that was able to face Pharisees, befriend traitors and love unconditionally. It is the kind of peace that must be only received. So technically, we should have this peace in us, and available to us right now. But logically we know that just because we have peace, does not guarantee that we fully experience it.

So how do we experience this peace that we apparently already have? This is where my fourth point becomes relevant. Culturally there are many belief systems that do not promote peace. Starting with probably the most common internal conflict; we as a society probably care too much about the opinions of others. Following Jesus is likely to have us unfavoured and unliked for at least some of the time. If not all the time. Paul goes so far as to say in Galatians 1:10 –

> "Am I now trying to win the approval of human beings, or of God? Or am I trying to please people? If I were still trying to please people, I would not be a servant of Christ."

Paul is talking to other believers here. Following the plan of God, might have other Christians disapproving of you too. And yet, we as believers, are often deluding ourselves into believing that it is possible to please God and man always. But as long as we believe our purpose is to please people, instead of God; we will not have peace. This is an anti-peace producing belief. You will create internal conflict, and you will have a substandard relationship with God. This is not profitable, and it does not ultimately produce peace. So if you really want peace, you are probably going to have to do something about this belief.

So whilst peace is available to us via the Spirit, our ability to appropriate peace determines our experience of peace, which is directly affected by the beliefs and illusions.

If you are genuinely disillusioned, you probably really wish you had a measure of peace right now. But there is a good chance that you have tried to resolve your disillusionment by addressing external factors. There is nothing outside of yourself, other than God, that will ever give you peace. Peace is an internal experience. It can only be resolved internally. I'm not suggesting that some factors external to you haven't needed to change. You probably did need to quit that job, move cities, or break up with your girlfriend. And you may have attained a measure of peace for having done that. But real peace, the kind that keeps you grounded in any and every situation, comes from the Spirit when you allow Him full access to your mindsets. In the next activity you will have a chance to start identifying those beliefs and illusions that have made it difficult to experience the peace He has already given you.

THE DISILLUSIONMENT INVENTORY

This next tool is the key practical process I undertook to heal from dis-illusionment. It's a structured reflection process that I drew up during my devotional time, whilst I was in the midst of my most significant time of disillusionment. The intention behind this table is to reveal the underlying causes of our disillusionment. In my experience, disillusion-ment is rarely just one illusion. It's a variety of mini-thoughts and beliefs that culminate into one overriding feeling and mindset. Through this inventory you will have an opportunity to view all the subsets of your disillusioning thoughts, and begin to tie up loose ends that have been disturbed. There are a few things that I would encourage you through this process:

- It is only as effective as your ability to be honest and trans-parent with yourself. Resist the temptation to deny issues that might come up, it only extends the time required to find meaning.
- It may take more than one sitting to do this well. Reflection requires time and patience. You may need to put an hour aside without distraction, to really think about your response to the questions.
- The place of prayer in this process cannot be discounted. It is primarily a process of focused conversation with God. Ask

other people to pray for you also - you can only benefit from more prayer.

• If you find you can't answer a question, don't stress or panic. Just move onto the questions that you can answer. Come back to it later with a fresh set of eyes.

With all that said, it's now time to take a glance at the Disillusionment Inventory.

The Disillusionment Inventory				
What am I disillusioned about?	What did I expect to see or thought would happen?	What might God have wanted me to see instead?	Why would He want me to see this?	Can this be validated in Scripture?

I know, it doesn't look like much. But the questions, and the order in which you answer them are the focal point of this process. These questions have been deliberately devised to carry you through to a conclusion. None of this is done without the consideration of God and His thoughts, which means that you have more of a chance to arrive at the conclusion that He wants you to gain.

A note: there is a copy of this table in the Appendix of this book, which you can copy as many times as you want. And you can also download a PDF from my website.

So let's begin.

COLUMN 1

What am I disillusioned about?

The first step is to identify the specific areas we are disillusioned by. For some of us it's really easy, we know exactly what disillusions us. But in this process it helps to get as detailed as you can about that disillusionment. Think about the statements you have made to close friends when sharing your feelings, what have you said specifically? For instance, if you are disillusioned about church, what exactly disillusions you?

Interestingly, for myself a significant area of disillusionment was about me. On one occasion when I was filling out this inventory, I wrote "I thought I was a better leader. I thought I would be able to change the culture." All throughout my leadership journey I had been told principles that would bring change and unity. I had used these principles in my secular jobs with incredible success. But then I came to the church and I wasn't able to bring that kind of change. I had no idea that I felt this way, and it is an example of a subset of my disillusionment. It wasn't necessarily the main issue, but it was an issue that contributed to the disillusionment and my fear of jumping right back into church and ministry again.

If you are struggling to identify the specific disillusionments, have a chat with a friend and talk about the area of disillusionment in general. Write down all the statements you have made whilst talking about that topic. Anyone of those statements could point to a more specific source of disillusionment.

COLUMN 2

What did I expect to see or thought would happen?

Note the specific disillusioning thought, then expand on that thought in more detail by answering the question in Column 2. This question is meant to draw out of the vision you had, that has been brought into question. Be as descriptive as you can be about the way you thought life would work out, it's important to see all in this step. Using the example from above, I sincerely believed that if I was a good enough leader that I could help staff members work together and care for each other in an environment where there had been significant mistrust. I sincerely believed that every conversation I had with staff could be a catalyst for unity and I made it my responsibility, because I was a leader.

This can be an interesting stage, because it may be the first time you've ever put to paper exactly what your expectations were. It can be painful to consider those things that you dreamed of, so give yourself some time and grace. And keep a tissue box nearby.

COLUMN 3

What might God have wanted me to see instead?

This next question is intended to define the gap between your expectations and what actually happened. This response to this question may get ugly and it may get you down...temporarily. Don't be afraid of the real answers to this question. It is a necessary step in moving toward the next question, that is significantly helpful in healing disillusionment. For the example I have mentioned in this section, when I came to this question my answer was quite depressing. What I actually discovered was that I wasn't enough. I wasn't enough of a leader to bring about the kind of change that was necessary. It was tough to come to terms with this, because I wanted to believe that I could fix anything. I wanted to believe I was an inspiring leader and that no challenge was too big for me. But reality told me something quite different.

COLUMN 4

Why would God have wanted me to see this?

This question is where the deeper reflection is required, but it's also where there is the greatest hope for a breakthrough. It reminds us that God has a purpose in our disillusionment. He wants to realign our beliefs and our illusions. And the only way to progress toward a realignment, is to ask ourselves His reasons for revealing His truth to us.

Initially I couldn't see any logical reason for God having revealed to me that I wasn't enough as a leader. I concluded that God had simply not given me the responsibility or the authority to change the church. He only wanted me to do what He had asked me to do. I know my desire to bring healing to different staff members was noble, but no leader in my position and with my authority could have changed what was happening. And that's because only God could change what was happening there.

Just make sure in answering this question that you seek God fervently. If you are still struggling to answer this question, it may be time to involve other parties in the conversation.

COLUMN 5

Can this be validated in scripture?

The process isn't complete until we answer this question. Because our conviction about why God wanted you to see another way, isn't solidified until it is compared with scripture and what He says. This part of the process can be hard, in that our understanding and knowledge of scripture can be at least a perceived limitation. But if you are unsure how to answer this question, as always, first pray. Then, take it to someone you know who gleans wisdom from the Word well.

For myself, the answer I found that validated my previous assumptions in Column 4 was that 'God will build His church' (Matthew 16:15). It was never my responsibility to change that church, because it is His church. And whilst I could read every leadership book and apply different principles and concepts, the only biblical leadership principle that applied when God sent me to this church, was that I be faithful and obey only that which He had asked me to do.

Be careful in this step, not to simply apply a common Christian statement that you heard in a sermon or social media. The goal is not to find any answer. It's to find THE answer for your specific scenario. If you are struggling still to find an answer for this one, again, just pray and give it some time. Come back to it when you are in a different mood. But don't give up, God will reveal the truth in due time.

If you've come this far, it means you are at the end of the process. You may find you need to do this several times. I certainly have! Sometimes you can only handle so much at one time, and God is patient to reveal things when we are in the right time to deal with it. You can always do this process in a group with trusted people too, if you are finding it hard to get to those deeper places.

I must caution you, you may feel sad at the outcome of this process. But that doesn't mean it was incorrect. It can be really confronting to map out all your hurts on a piece of paper. But you should feel some kind of relief either immediately after, or in the coming days. If you don't go back and have a look at your answers to Column 4. Were you unreasonably harsh on yourself? Was this what the average person would have responded to this question? Because that question isn't intended to be your perspective of yourself, it's meant to be God's perspective. There is a window in this question to reveal our own self-deprecating thoughts. So just make sure that your answer wasn't filtered through your own insecurities.

If you discover anything that you might need to repent of, make sure that you take time with God. We need to put our illusions completely to rest by giving them over to God.

I would love to hear how this whole process was for you, so please send feedback. My prayer is that you are getting closer and closer to freedom from fear, pain, anger and every other result that disillusionment has brought to your life.

Jonah

It is hard to reconcile how dramatically different the story of Jonah is to me now compared with what I understood as an eight year old child. It is truly a remarkable story and not necessarily because of the way God involved a whale in His masterplan. Jonah clearly had something against the Ninevites. They were enemies of the Jewish people, and God was asking Jonah to go directly to them giving them an opportunity to repent. You see, it's not until the end of the book that you realise that Jonah's response to God to run in the complete opposite direction was not induced by fear. Nor was it because he was a rebellious person by nature and simply didn't want to obey God. It was induced by His knowledge of God. He knew that God was merciful, and he simply could not fathom the possibility that God desired to offer mercy to the Ninevites, a Gentile nation that was violent and cruel. It would seem that Jonah did not believe the Ninevites were worthy of the mercy God would give, in fact He wanted the destruction to come to pass. The thought of the Ninevites repentance caused him to long for death. And so after Jonah ran from God, he is thrown into the sea, is captured by a whale and spat out, and finally he goes to the Ninevites. He prophesies, they repent and he sits outside the city lamenting and watching what is to come of God's mercy. Whilst he watches he remarks to God that he has a right to be angry as he simultaneously hopes for death.

WHAT ARE THE SIGNS OF DISILLUSIONMENT?

The most significant sign that Jonah may have been disillusioned is the fact that he runs. The first thing that often happens for a person who is supremely disillusioned is that they run away. They get as far away as they can from the source of their disillusionment, because being close threatens them. Whenever some kind of major conflict happens at a church, those who are affected will often run far from church because they don't have the resources in that emotional state to deal with the frequent reminders that they've seen something they can't unsee. Sometimes it's fear, sometimes it's anxiety, but whatever it is for that individual they often can't psychologically handle their foundations being rocked. In this story, Jonah didn't just run he ran in the opposite direction. He was trying to get as far as he could from anything that would remotely remind him of Nineveh and possibly of God. If he only wanted to disobey, he certainly didn't need to run that far away. He could have stayed where he was, and it still would have been disobedient. Instead the emotion he feels about this request is so intense that he must run as far as he can in the opposite direction. His lack of obedience quite possibly stemmed from the fact that he could not reconcile how God could offer mercy to a nation that had caused so much harm.

The second sign is his anger. Jonah was angry at God and at the circumstances. The redemption and repentance of the Ninevite people was good news both for the Israelite people and the Ninevites. It meant that there would be no more enmity and brutality. It might even mean peace amongst the nations. And of course it meant an end to the destruction of the Ninevites. But Jonah wasn't at all happy! Because he still thought it was unjust and unfair that Nineveh received grace.

WHAT CAN WE LEARN FROM THE STORY OF JONAH?

1.   God's mercy cannot be controlled

Though Jonah could not understand how God could give mercy to the Ninevites, he was repeatedly benefiting from God's mercy throughout the story. The first merciful act of God, was that Jonah was born an Israelite. We forget sometimes that we don't really have much of a say in where, when and to whom we are born. Secondly, God chose Jonah to be a prophetic voice. Whilst that is not at all an easy task, it is surely an honourable one.

Then Jonah runs, and the storm hits. We wouldn't ordinarily class it as such, but the storm was God's mercy too. Mercy doesn't always come in the form of material blessing. It can sometimes come in the form of a storm or a desert that pushes us to levels of faith that we didn't know we could have. God wasn't letting Jonah just run away into anonymity without facing some misaligned illusions that were preventing him from being a greater vessel for God.

Despite all the mercy, when it came to the Ninevites he wanted a say in who, how and to what extent God's mercy should be administered. We actually don't get that right. We can't possess God's mercy and restrict it's access to others. We receive it like a gift. It was freely given to us, and undeservedly so. To think that because we have arrived at some kind of spiritual maturity, that our deservedness of mercy increases is to misunderstand mercy altogether.

It can be really hard to grapple with the mercy that God gives to those who have hurt you, or have done wrong. It's not an easy fact to consider. But in your frustrations you can still choose to humble yourself before God and recognise how undeserving you are of the mercy you have been given. Focus on that. I know it might seem unfair, but none of us get what is fair. Grace and mercy aren't fair. They aren't based on deservedness, it's based on the purity of God's love. Grow in your capacity to love your enemies, as you consider the love that has been poured out for you.

2.   God is patient with those who are disillusioned

In most other parts of Old Testament scripture, when someone disobeyed God, very serious punishment would unfold. For Saul, when he took it upon himself to complete tasks only a priest could, he basically lost his kingship. But Jonah has very obviously and overtly rejected the direction of God and yet God gives him a second chance?

Yes it does seem strange. It tells me that God is very patient. He probably understood that this was a significant challenge for Jonah. We'll never know, but maybe the Ninevites had done something personal to him. Maybe they hurt his family. Maybe they even killed his family. We don't get enough of a backstory to be able to know for sure. But if his prejudice toward them was personally motivated, it would surely change what was once deemed 'disobedience'. If you are in a place of disillusionment, I can assure you that God is patient with you too. He'll give you time, because He is committed to you for life. Even when you aren't. Even when you give up on Him. His covenant is lifelong, and it's unconditional. He is patient for you to participate with Him in receiving healing and a renewed hope. Even if you are being disobedient and falling into sin, He is still patient waiting for you to turn even one degree toward Him. Just like the prodigal son, even a slight turn in His direction will cause you to see Him running full speed toward you, only to discover He has been running with you all your life.

3.   God still has plans for you

God was persistent with Jonah. He still wanted Jonah to speak to the Ninevites despite his initial response. Jonah thought he couldn't handle it, but God knew he could though he fell in a metaphorical heap of self-pity at the end of it. See, what would have happened to Jonah if he had absconded on the ship without consequence? What would he have become? Sometimes we escape to a place of perceived safety, because we are afraid. That is understandable, for a time. But where will that leave us in the long run? Would Jonah be able to look back on his life and be proud of the choices he made?

The biggest risk personally to Jonah was that He would never face this prejudice that he appeared to have against the Ninevites. In some ways maintaining this prejudice was of greater value to him than God. He was willing to disobey God to avoid dealing with it. Does that not sound so familiar? We all have hang ups, and areas that we would rather run from than face. But the issues we actually do run from have more power over us than we care to acknowledge. Anything that is emotive enough to change our direction besides God, is ultimately our master. Matthew 6:24 tells us this:

> *"No one can serve two masters. Either you will hate the one and love the other, or you will be loyal to the one and have contempt for the other."*

You know, it's not really my style to take a black and white approach to matters of life. But this is one area that I do. Ultimately either God is your master or He is not. You don't need to feel too bad if you are still on that journey of making Him Lord. Because God is really patient. As long as we fully committed to being His disciple. To put it quite simply, God will continue to offer opportunities that direct us to a deeper and more committed relationship with Him. It's not a power play on God's behalf. He does this because what He has for us is immersed in grace and goodness. The things that oppose His Lordship in our life, are often not full of that same grace and goodness. God would not have genuinely loved Jonah if he simply allowed him to remain in a state of running away.

God had a plan and He wasn't going to give up on Jonah, even though Jonah had given up. God has a plan for you, even if you have given up. It may be really hard to summon hope right now, but I want to assure you of one really important thing: God puts His hope in you. In fact He always hopes for you. In the famous 'love' passage 1 Corinthians 13 it says:

> *"Love is patient, love is kind. It does not envy, it does not boast, it is not proud. It does not dishonour others, it is not self-seeking, it is not easily angered, it keeps no record of wrongs. Love does not delight in evil but rejoices with the truth. It always protects, always trusts, **always hopes**, always perseveres"* (emphasis mine)

It is a quality of love, to hope for others. You might not know whether you are capable of growing beyond your disillusionment, but God absolutely believes you can. He trusts you and He perseveres for you. He never stops hoping for you.

CHAPTER 5

One step at a time

When I was pregnant with my daughter, I received lots and lots of advice that sometimes I never asked for. One of the best pieces of advice came from a friend was not to have too many expectations about life and the baby in the first six weeks. It was such incredibly wise advice! That first six weeks was completely unpredictable as every parent would have experienced. My daughter wouldn't sleep in a bassinet, and I had to sit in a recliner and hold her while she slept. Then I had to go back and forth to the hospital for help with nursing, a jaundice concern, and my own health issues. Even though I was warned that I wouldn't get a lot of sleep, it still was a shock that I could run on such low resources. I didn't get any significant amount of time to do housework or to cook meals. Ordinarily, that would have stressed me out and made me feel overwhelmed. But because of the wise advice of my friend, I wasn't so phased by the chaos. I could handle every unpredictable situation thrown at me, because my expectations were fluid.

My observation is that when you are going through something new, it is so helpful to have someone tell you what to expect, even if that's not to expect too much. It calms our fears when someone tells us that what we are going through is normal. The same can be said of disillusionment. Being able to have an idea of what is normal, can help immeasurably. In some ways, this is what I am doing by writing this book. But even after the Disillusionment Inventory, there is still a potential for situations to return to the way they were. This next chapter will address barriers that pose a threat to your progress through disillusionment. They are less obvious, and hence why they can be a real risk to healing.

WISDOM OVER FEAR

1. Expect multiple layers and delay in the healing process.

> When I used to work in Workers Compensation insurance, we referred to a manual when making a cost estimate at the outset of a claim. This manual held the average timeframe for recovery for every injury common to workplaces. We used these timeframes to work out when the progress of a case was indicating a risk of going pear-shaped. Although it was fairly common for a case to go longer than noted in the injury time frames, it was fairly unusual for a case to go significantly shorter. It is possible, but that was not my experience. Maybe a week or two out of twelve weeks, but not two months. So here is a fairly universal truth; with the exception of God's supreme intervention, the healing process has a timeframe of its own. You don't get to dictate the timeframe, you can only participate in the healing process to make sure that you arrive at the end, instead of it being perpetually unfinished. Real healing takes time. And often it's multi-layered. Think about a physical injury. The priority is healing the source of the injury, as well as protecting the wound and preventing infection. The body has its own inbuilt mechanisms that kickstart the healing process. Therefore, if a person's immunity is impaired, this process is affected. Stress, pressure, and rest all affect the healing process. Healing is multi-layered.

Additionally the more complicated the injury, the more multi-layered the healing process.

Innumerable people have told me that "I should be over this by now". The only thing that this statement tells me is that people have expectations about the healing process. And that these expectations are often unfounded. I'm not sure what we are basing our expectations on, but we seem to often be wrong. People expect that time genuinely takes away their pain. Time does help sometimes. But only if we have tended appropriately to a heart wound. Again, in the case of a physical injury we know that time will eventually heal a laceration. That is only if the appropriate medical treatment was applied in the early stages: cleaning the wound, applying appropriate ointments, and covering it. If not done, that wound is not healing. Give yourself a break, allow your heart to heal without putting unnecessary expectations on it.

2. You may want to slow your pace on launching into the 'new normal'.

Because healing is multi-layered, you often don't know the layers that lie beneath. It would be wise not to launch forward by signing up for different roles or activities as soon as you start feeling a bit better. The possibility of jumping in naively without wisdom and discernment, and regressing further in your disillusionment is really dangerous. It's one of the biggest reasons friends will advise you against a relationship after a major breakup. You probably still have baggage even if you aren't aware of it, and no relationship is going to help you get over that. And the further damage that another bad relationship could bring, has the potential to make you so much worse off than you were in the first relationship. It's the cumulative effect of disillusionment that often has us giving up. I have a few friends who have gone through some church hurts. And often when they have taken a bit of time away from serving in church, and then jumped right back in without taking the time to heal significantly from their previous disillusionments, they've ended up either leaving church or giving up on faith altogether. Now I know that church is a significant part of faith, but you can heal your relationship with church when you still have your faith in God. But it's difficult to heal your relationship with God when you don't have much faith in God. Give yourself a chance to really heal.

3. But taking some steps are important.

If you know that a measure of healing has happened to you, do something with it. But do something small. It's better to do something small than nothing at all. Our hearts can also be influenced by activation. We aren't hermits of internal experiences disconnected from society. We interact with our environment everyday. For a person who has a hospitality gift and likes cooking, making someone a meal blesses them as much as the person eating the meal. Activation contributes to our experiences. We learn and heal by doing sometimes, it's more about how much we do that can be a risk to the healing process. You don't need to jump straight back into the dating scene, you could just join a small group or start socialising a bit more. You may not go straight back into pastoring and leading, just be on the welcome team or make someone a meal. You don't need to move back in with your wife straight away after separating, why not start counselling or go on a date with each other. There are always small steps we can take, that don't place the entire process at risk.

4.   Be intentional with internal resistance.

If you start taking small steps, you will notice an occasional internal resistance. Maybe it's fear. Maybe it's just feelings of vulnerability. Maybe it's anger. Whatever you call it, it's a discomforting feeling that sometimes makes you want to run for the hills. Here's the thing about emotions: they are an indicator. They don't necessarily tell the whole truth about a situation. They reflect what might be going on under the surface in response to a situation. When I started at my new church, I had a day where I started to feel like I couldn't be a part of the congregation anymore. I felt like running away and never returning. I projected anger as I vented to my husband, but after a day I realised I was just feeling afraid. I was afraid of going through the pain and hurt that I had been through before. I had to keep reminding myself that this church was different, and that at this time of vulnerability I had to keep walking forward. This was where God wanted us to be. If I had listened to that fear, I would have missed out on the incredible community that I now have. And that would've been a terrible shame. You will have those moments where discomfort happens. My encouragement to you, is to take a step back, honour the feeling, try to understand the source of that feeling and take it to God in prayer. You could take out the Disillusionment Inventory again. Or you might want to talk to someone you trust. Whatever you do, don't pretend that it didn't happen. Don't blame other people for that feeling. Don't just get locked into that feeling assuming that it's telling you the truth without trying to understand the deeper motivator for that feeling. To ignore it, could undo all the progress you have made.

5.   You will still see anomalies from time to time.

> There usually is a measure of truth to all illusions. Equally, there is a measure of untruth to every illusion. Which means you are going to see things that could reaffirm the disillusioning thoughts you've had before. You might still see aspects about men that, as a woman, makes you want to give up on all men. Just like men will see things about women that make them want to give up on women! You won't stop seeing those aspects that could get you in that place of questioning again. I still occasionally hear statements on Facebook or Instagram that cause me to wonder about church. But these days I am much more prepared for these anomalies, and recognise that there is still so much good in the church. I can see the sinful choices of believers and balance that with my knowledge of the goodness in believers too, without wanting to throw in the towel.

I want to reassure you that there will come a time when you will be able to wake up and feel released in your heart and mind from the disillusionment of the past. The timeframe differs for every person. Going through this process is not going to create resolution for every gap you see in life and the world. This is an impossibility. Some situations are meant to create a psychological conundrum because they return us to a place of awe and humility at the mystery of God. Even though you might still see those gaps, you don't have to feel controlled by them. As a society, we could afford to get a bit more comfortable with gaps. They are everywhere. There is plenty that doesn't make sense in the world, and whilst we have multitudes of people out there seeking to understand those gaps there is a good chance that we will not arrive at the truth in this lifetime. But we can still live. I am personally trying to become more comfortable with saying "I don't know" and working out whether I even need to know certain things to keep doing what

I am doing. I'm not talking about blind faith. That's not what I am advocating for here. I'm talking about the fact that even after all of our searching, when we come up with a situation that we can't quite reconcile we can still have peace even when we don't know. The process of healing from disillusionment increased my capability of holding my opinions loosely. Consequently this increased God's ability to change how I thought about certain aspects of life, that had previously held foundational positions. Instead, my relationship with Him and what I knew about Him became my foundations. Rather than my formula (that is often **not** based on strictly biblical ideas like we all assume they are) for how the world works.

WHAT DO I DO WITH TRIGGERS?

'Triggers' is a term that probably gets a little bit overused these days. I've had a lot to do with people with mental health issues, and genuine triggers can be devastating. It could have them in full blown panic attacks. It could have them crying and losing sleep. It can reaggravate a psychological episode and have them reliving past trauma. Unfortunately, the term has entered the colloquial vernacular so much so that any form of discomfort about a situation is termed a 'trigger'. Now, there are definitely people I have met that just appear judgmental and critical that call their gossipy episodes a 'trigger'.

At the end of the day, if you are concerned about any feeling, it is wise to talk to a qualified professional. If any of these triggers cause you to sin (angry outbursts, gossiping) even if it doesn't cause any obvious psychological distress, it's still worth talking to someone. Maybe a pastor, or even a trained professional. If we are truly committed to our faith, we don't want to allow ourselves to use a trigger as an excuse for sin. We ought to understand the underlying factors that may be contributing to such a reaction, because that kind of reaction deserves some attention too.

Additionally, make a note of the specific circumstances you are feeling triggered by. Try and get as accurate as you can on the source of your trigger. Even if it's just a 'look' that someone gives you. That can be really helpful information. Being able to isolate the source of your triggers will go a long way to helping yourself and professionals you engage with and in your healing process. When I was still healing, the thing that would 'trigger' me was watching a meeting leader during a service. It would often distract me for the rest of the service. When I finally worked it out, it gave me a chance to really investigate why that specific part of a service was triggering these anxious feelings. I was able to isolate it down to a specific experience I had with meeting leading, that was unresolved. I met with a counsellor and began talking through that specific experience. In the meantime, whenever I saw a meeting leader on stage I just tried to be somewhere else in the service or I looked down. I tried not to talk about it to other people, with the exception of my trusted few. In time, I was able to go to church and not be bothered by the meeting leader and anything they were doing. But all of that happened because I took note of what kept triggering me.

If you have made progress through your disillusionment, it's really important to protect the progress you've made. Don't be fearful, but be wise. That's really what this whole chapter is about. If you feel disillusionment creeping up again, go straight back to the Inventory as soon as you can.

In the next chapter, we talk about a type of disillusionment that is particularly difficult. Disillusionment relating to the injustices of prejudice and poverty.

CASE STUDY 5
Joseph

Outside of Jesus, it would be difficult to find someone in the Bible with a harder life than Joseph. The exception is probably Job. As much as the story of Joseph is uplifting, it is also dreadfully sorrowful to watch the story unfold. Just when you think he is going well, another event prevents him from prospering. Even when he finally sees his brothers again, you don't necessarily feel like 'he won'. You feel the overwhelming sense of grief that he carried from the day his brothers decided to sell him off. I've heard lots of preachers talk about the fact that Joseph had a dream. Yes, he did have a literal dream in which a vision from God was revealed while sleeping. But we don't necessarily see any proof that this dream was what Joseph also wanted. I don't think it's as simple to say that Joseph was faithful to the dream, he was just incredibly faithful to God. He humbly persevered through whatever God put before him.

WHAT ARE THE SIGNS OF DISILLUSIONMENT?

In the story of Joseph, it is really hard to separate possible disillusion- ment from mourning. There are many points that could just be Joseph in despair. In fact, Joseph doesn't actually say a lot throughout his entire story, which certainly makes it tougher. So whilst I offer up these points to you, I'm not as convinced as the other case studies that this is a definite disillusionment. The first sign we see is after he is thrown in jail and meets Pharaoh's officials in custody. In Genesis 40:14, he asks the cupbearer to mention him to the Pharaoh so that he could be let out of prison. Now who would enjoy prison? Of course, everyone would want to get out. But the next verse is the first time we actually hear him talk about his predicament:

> *"I was forcibly carried off from the land of the Hebrews, and even here I have done nothing to deserve being put in a dungeon"* Genesis 40:15

Joseph is not silent about the injustices that he has faced, and furthermore he wants out. In this statement, it doesn't necessarily give us a window into whether he even thought about the dream when he asks to be mentioned to the Pharaoh. He just wants out.

Joseph's situation completely changes in Genesis 41. He goes on to interpret Pharaoh's dream, and is established as a leader over Egypt. Pharaoh also gives him a wife, and by verse 50 he also has two sons before the famine hits. Interestingly though, he gives his sons some unusual names. His firstborn son's name 'Manasseh' was given meaning 'God has made me forget all my troubles and everyone in my father's family'. And his son Ephraim was named to mean 'God has made me fruitful in this land of my grief'. These statements again, really demonstrate that the past had troubled him and that he associated his time in Egypt with pain and sorrow. It's difficult to believe he had literally forgotten his family and troubles when his son's name was devised in light of his past. But 'Manassah' likely meant 'forget'. Which might indicate some contentment with his life, causing him to forget his longing for his family. And though he had arrived at a place of blessing, he still called Egypt the land of his grief.

Sadly, Joseph cries four times in this latter part of the story. In Genesis 45:2 after seeing his brothers a second time we learn that Joseph wept so loudly that all of Pharaoh's household heard. The presence of his brothers brought so much pain and anguish that he simply couldn't control it.

So you see it is rather difficult to identify what might have been disillusionment and what might have been grief. The only thing that really does raise some questions about Joseph's state of mind, and potentially the presence of disillusionment, is that for seven years, he is in charge of Egypt and he never once returns home? He doesn't even send a messenger! He could have sent a spy, to see if his father was still alive. Instead, he loses all contact with the past, including those he loved. Grief may be responsible for this, but it may suggest disillusionment.

WHAT CAN WE LEARN FROM THE STORY OF JOSEPH?

1.   Just focus on the next thing

Imagine what it would be like for Joseph to have been in jail. He had no idea if he would ever be released. Things really didn't seem to work out the way one would expect. He went backwards, and backwards and backwards...until he finally was catapulted forward! Nobody would have seen this coming. And such are God's plans. They won't happen in a straight line. Where you are right now, as far as it seems to be from your desired future, could be the closest you've ever been to it. Maybe you found yourself just like me, at home, middle aged and wondering exactly how a vision was ever going to come true. I was the furthest I could possibly be from the things I believed God had for me. I'm still pretty far if I'm honest. But I have resolved in my heart that His plan for me is going to be unusual and unlike anyone else I know. And that is a good thing. If I could predict the path of God, I would not value it. I have come to a place now, that I don't actually feel like I need to know anymore. I just keep focusing on the next thing God tells me to do. I still have my days where I doubt, but I just keep focusing on the next thing. When I was in the midst of my really severe disillusionment, I had only one thing that I knew God wanted me to do. That was to write my first book, Ministry Stinks. So much good came out of that process for me, including the vision for this book. You might be tempted to want to change your present circumstances, but instead...just focus on doing the next task He has put before you to do.

2. God is faithful

God was so incredibly faithful to Joseph. In the cistern, at Potiphar's house, in the jail, with the Pharaoh. Yes it was a long drawn out series of events. But every bit of it was integral to the next step. He would not even have had an opportunity to interpret the Pharaoh's dream if he hadn't first been in the jail. He wouldn't have been in jail, if it wasn't for Potiphar's wife. And he wouldn't have been in Potiphar's house if it weren't for his brothers. God knew the events that would happen, and he perfectly steered it so that Joseph's dream would be actualised. God was with Joseph at every step of the way and gave him favour though he found himself in such dreadful circumstances. God never forgot the vision.

CHAPTER 6

Prejudice and Poverty

Netflix released a remarkable series early in 2019 called "The Way They See Us". It presents the story of five young black men who were charged and convicted of the brutal sexual assault of Trisha Meili, a 28 year old white female, that took place in New York's Central Park on 19th April 1989. The director did an incredible job of presenting the arrest and interview of the five young men who were manipulated and badgered throughout the investigation. It is downright disgusting to watch how prejudice and manipulation fester in this story, to find young boys in a predicament well beyond what they deserved. And all the while they were not responsible for a single part of the incident. The boys spent between six and thirteen years in prison for a crime they didn't commit. They were exonerated when the real perpetrator confessed in 2002. Consider how many years they lost in their youth because of this mammoth injustice.

Imagine my shock when I realised that this was all based on a true story. I actually felt sick to my stomach. I had never heard of the story of the Central Park Five or the Central Park Jogger. I was only six years old at the time and I am not sure how publicised it would have been here in Australia. For days, I continued to think about the five. I Googled and read everything I could find about the case and the young boys involved.

Oprah Winfrey did a special that was featured on Netflix also, with the actual five young men and the director and it was truly eye opening. Whilst all of them had created a life of sorts, it could hardly be said that they had simply 'moved on'. One of the five men sincerely struggled to talk about everything that happened to him. And who could possibly blame him? Racism took so much away from him. From all of them.

This chapter wasn't a part of the original plan in this book. But how could I really delve into the topic of disillusionment without talking about some of the toughest most disillusioning contemporary circumstances to be found. I'm talking about prejudice and poverty, both a very particular kind of injustice. Disillusionment borne of such types of injustice is by far the hardest to recover from.

Why would we need to talk about such specific types of injustice separately? It is true that in every disillusionment there is a portion of injustice. When a spouse has an affair, a portion of the battle is the injustice of it. When a child doesn't want to talk to you anymore, some of the pain relates to the injustice of that. When a church relationship goes sour, injustice surely would have a part to play in your frustration and anger. But there are certain kinds of circumstances that are an all encompassing injustice. For instance, when it comes to any kind of prejudice where people are ill-treated because of a quality that they are born with, it's all injustice. Not just a portion. To go through the usual processes presented here in this book, for example the section titled 'Recognise the part you played' in Chapter 4, is a completely irrelevant step for someone on the receiving end of injustice.

I am definitely not going to suggest that I have the answers to all the questions that would arise in this topic. There is no easy solution either. Anything that I suggest in this book, are simply ideas that might work. Emphasis on 'might'. I offer them to you, the person who has suffered at the hands of injustice. I hope it helps, but I also understand if it doesn't.

THE FACTS ABOUT INJUSTICE

- It's a reality

  There are people in this world who discount the experiences of those who are in the minority or disadvantaged. It's not always because they are prejudiced. It can be hard to comprehend that there is inequality when it hasn't been your personal experience. The fact is, the Bible frequently provides us stories and examples of prejudice. When we hear the story of the Good Samaritan, we take away the challenging message to love our neighbours. But for the people at that time, it is possible that the focal point of the story was the implication that the hero could be a Samaritan. Or worse yet, that a Samaritan could be of value. There was great animosity between the Jewish people and the Samaritans. It wasn't just a conflict, it was nationalism. And Jesus was simultaneously challenging the people of that day about loving their neighbour, including those who are despised.

  Even Jonah demonstrates the story of a man who would rather not see a people group receive mercy because of their nationality. The Ninevites were enemies of the Israelites and in Jonah's mind it would have been unjust for the Ninevites to have been given mercy. Even if it is hard for some to comprehend that injustice is real by simply listening to the multitude of stories out there, open your eyes to scripture and you will see your fair share of injustice. It's real, and it is present in every generation.

- Justice is a significant part of every believer's calling.

  The Bible talks frequently about the mandate for every believer to participate in issues of justice. Unfortunately, Christians have often been the perpetrators of that very same injustice. But we were always supposed to advocate for those who were oppressed and disadvantaged. One thing I love about this millennial generation is that they do have an increased social conscience. Despite all the suggestions that this is a self-centred generation with their preoccupation with selfies and the like, they have shown that they care. This care often leads them to march and protest, which may at times seem misguided, but we must recognise it as a response to silence.

One of the typically oppressed demographics in Jesus' time were widows. They were systematically oppressed both legally and culturally. The laws at that time didn't acknowledge women without a husband. And therefore without a husband, a woman was vulnerable. Often widows would participate in prostitution because of this vulnerability. This is what makes the story of Tamar so staggering (Genesis 38). As with most women of her time, Tamar's validity as a person was primarily in her husband, and secondly in her ability to provide an heir. Tamar unfortunately marries Judah's son Er, who dies. None of which is her fault. Then Judah gives her brother-in-law, Onan, who customarily takes the responsibility to give her a child which would be Er's heir. But Onan does something so dishonourable to both his brother and Tamar, and deliberately sees to it that Tamar does not fall pregnant. Such an action attracted the wrath of God, and he was killed. She was then sent back to her home by Judah to be a widow until his last son came of age. Of course, Judah had no intention of allowing her to have access to the younger son assuming that Tamar was the cause of his two sons death. In this way, Judah also dishonours her and leaves her vulnerable. In a nutshell, Tamar then tricks Judah into sleeping with her and she has a child. Interestingly, when Judah realises what she has done he remarks, *"She is more righteous than I"*. I find it so interesting that whilst God intervenes to kill the two sons, and one in particular for his choice to restrict pregnancy with Tamar, at no point does God intervene in Tamar's plan to fall pregnant to Judah though it is deceptive. Now that certainly doesn't suggest that God approved of every choice in her plan, but it is interesting how God selectively intervenes in this story. God often favours those who are vulnerable and disadvantaged. He favoured Ruth, he favoured Rahab, he favoured Leah. I could go on. Being vulnerable attracts the favour of God.

There is evidence in the New Testament that caring for the widows is a critical area of strategy for those in the early church. The financial expenditure of the church factored in the widows and their care. The support of the widows was not only in word, but in action.

God probably does have a specific kind of compassion for the widow, and we ought to take note of this demographic today. But it is also likely that such passages reflect God's desire for the body of Christ to prioritise the needs of those who are vulnerable and disadvantaged. When Jesus ushered in the children and declared that we must have child-like faith, He was declaring this in an era where infanticide was legal and entire societies were still in the practice of leaving a baby to die on garbage heaps outside the city walls. We are supposed to advocate, support practically and spiritually, those who are systematically and culturally disadvantaged just as Jesus advocated. Especially those in our community. This is the mandate of the church and it goes beyond our opinions or politics. It doesn't matter if you are single or married with children. We are to provide a safe place where oppression created by the cultural and legal structure is nullified.

None of this means that we are inappropriate and disrespectful in how we pursue justice, but it does mean we passionately pursue justice. We are all called to *'take care of the orphans and widows.'* (James 1:27)

Consider this, if the body of Christ had both corporately and individually taken it upon themselves to see justice as a part of their calling, what kind of change could be seen in this world? Is it possible that much of the injustices done in this world, would have progressed further had God's people been more active in pursuing justice for our fellow man?

JUSTICE IN GENERAL...

The scriptures have a lot to say on the subject of justice and God's heart on the matter and it is important to explore this before we speak more specifically about prejudice and poverty:

> *'He ensures that orphans and widows receive justice.*
> *He shows love to the foreigners living among you and*
> *gives them food and clothing. So you, too, must show*
> *love to foreigners, for you yourselves were once foreign-*
> *ers in the land of Egypt'.* Deuteronomy 10:18-19

When the Israelites were foreigners in another land, they weren't treated well. They were enslaved, in some cases forced to worship other gods (Shardarch, Meshech and Abednego) or they were the object of murderous threats (during Esther's reign). In typical counter-cultural fashion, this was not the desire of God in the community of His chosen people. He would have it that every foreigner in the Israelite community experienced the same citizenship and benefits as though there were no distinction between them.

> *He has shown you, O mortal, what is good.*
> *And what does the Lord require of you?*

To act justly and to love mercy
and to walk humbly with your God. Micah 6:8

The Lord requires us to act justly. That is to act in a way that is true and just to all. To those above us and those who serve us. It means that we don't oppress anyone, we give to those what they are due, to act equitably and hurt nobody in word or deed.

'The Lord loves righteousness and justice;
the earth is full of his unfailing love'. Psalm 33:5

God LOVES justice. As believers, we care about that which God cares about. We want to love what God loves. JUSTICE meets that criteria. To love God, therefore, is to love justice.

But you must return to your God;
maintain love and justice,
and wait for your God always. Hosea 12:6

God possibly couldn't be more direct. He wants us all to maintain love and justice amongst the communities in which we find ourselves.

There is plenty of oppression that exists today, but our middle class lives can shield us from responding. Slavery still exists. Oppressive laws and practices continue to oppress marginalised groups. The call to justice requires us to look beyond our comfortable lives and consider the experience of others, because personal experience doesn't negate our responsibility to seek justice.

PREJUDICE

Racism, sexism, and particularly any prejudice that has left a person experiencing negative consequences is simply awful. It's a pre-rejection and a pre-judgement that is completely based on personhood. The terrible reality is that many will suffer unfair consequences at the hand of another's' sinful choices. And these consequences can alter the trajectory of a person's life.

For the believers, there is no distinction:

> *There is neither Jew nor Greek, there is neither slave nor free, there is no male and female, for you are all one in Christ Jesus.* Galatians 3:28

Our diversity should be the cause for celebration. Diversity testifies again to the glory of God and His perfect wisdom as the Creator. However, those who experience prejudice can feel like they are cursed when society treats them, like that difference, is a cause for ill treatment. The reality is, that God demonstrated His creative genius when He gave us such unique features. So though you feel like you are cursed, be thankful for the way He made you. God chose you to bear His image, whether the world likes it or not. You need not feel ashamed, though the world seems to want to hide you. Know that He holds you up and rejoices over you in the heavenly realm. He applauds and celebrates you.

If you have been on the receiving end of prejudice, you need to know that the body of Christ collectively was meant to be more embracing. The prejudice you have experienced was supposed to be the concern of the church and we haven't always made it our problem.

Whenever any person...male, female, child, elderly, receives treatment that is less than the dignity and respect they deserve as an image bearer of God Almighty, it is affront to all. When one of us is devalued, all are devalued. We have been designed with honour and significance, by the hand of God, to reflect the very nature of God. No person has been created in error. Instead, every person is of divine design. Even if that person completely debases themselves with the most evil activities in which they could participate, it does not give me licence to see or treat them as anything less than God's masterpiece designed at the hand of the Father. Full of value, dignity, and honour. Whether they are a believer or not. We are all designed and created by God Almighty.

POVERTY

The Bible is very clear on the issue of poverty. It is also a big part of our calling as believers to help those in poverty. There was a time when I presumed that giving and serving those in poverty was optional. I understood that service to the poor was specifically for those called by God to serve in this way, whether financially or practically. But it is really difficult to maintain that belief when you read all that Jesus says in the Gospels and the Bible in general.

> *There will always be some in the land who are poor.*
> *That is why I am commanding you to share freely*
> *with the poor and with other Israelites in need.*
> Deuteronomy 15:11 (NLT)

Poverty is often described as cyclical, and incredibly hard to break. Jesus always brings hope. But more people are experiencing poverty everyday, as the verse above suggests. Job loss, marital breakdown, mental health issues, injury or illness and more recently a global pandemic. It's interesting to note in this verse that God is unconcerned about the reason for their poverty. Sometimes our Western minds reason 'they did it to themselves', that they are just experiencing the consequences of their poor choices. But if God had operated on this logic none of us would be saved. Their 'choices' should not limit our response. Sharing freely is about who we are as much as it is about another's needs being met. It testifies to our nature, and our willingness to be obedient to God regardless of the outcome. God's desire in this passage was for the Israelite community. His chosen people would be the conduit of provision. And this still applies today. There are numerous passages in the New Testament that demonstrate this continued priority of the poor. Our response to the poverty induced injustice, is to share what we have. Not only the poor, but those believers who are also in need. This isn't a job only for your pastor. This isn't about tithing, and it doesn't mean that personal responsibility is negated because your church has a community arm. It isn't only for the pastoral care team. It is shared by all of us who call ourselves a part of God's family.

Now most of us would help out with a meal or two when some-one has an urgent need. But this is going well beyond that. It's talking about people in chronic poverty. Maybe they won't ever escape poverty. And whether our money makes the impact we would desire it to have, we are still called to share. This is absolutely mind boggling! All of us think of how our dollar can be more effective. I was recently encouraging a friend to get themselves a Soda Stream because it is better value than buying the copious amounts of sparkling water they consume. We are considerate with our own money, because we are mindful of our future needs. We reason that we ought to give in a way that is forward thinking and leads to a better outcome overall for the greatest number of people. But this is not supposed to be at the expense of simply sharing what we have with the poor and those around us in need. This is a radical notion because at the heart of it is another principle that the Western world is hesitant to preach. The Bible affirms frequently that everything in this world belongs to Him. That's right, EVERYTHING! The money you earn is actually His. The house you come home to, coincidentally sits on a piece of land that belongs to Him. The council doesn't own that land. It's God's land, since He created the earth. The company you work for doesn't own the resources used to make their product. It has come from some physical source that originated in God's creation. WE are not our own. Sure, we were 'made' by our parents...but God put that whole process of reproduction in place so that humankind could procreate. We have nothing that has magically appeared. It all began with a seed that God planted. All of it is on loan to us to steward, but none of it belongs to us. We reason that we worked for it, therefore we earned it. But this is not consistent with scripture.

- 1 Corinthians 10:26
  The earth and all that is in it belong to the Lord (referencing Psalm 24:1)

- Colossians 1:16
  Because all things were created by him:
  both in the heavens and on the earth,
  the things that are visible and the things that are invisible.
  Whether they are thrones or powers,
  or rulers or authorities,
  all things were created through him and for him.

- Psalm 50:12
  Even if I were hungry, I wouldn't tell you
  because the whole world and everything in it already belong to me.

- Haggai 2:8
  The silver and the gold belong to me, says the Lord of heavenly forces.

- Deuteronomy 8:17-18
  Don't think to yourself, My own strength and abilities have produced all this prosperity for me. Remember

the Lord your God! He's the one who gives you the strength to be prosperous in order to establish the covenant he made with your ancestors—and that's how things stand right now.

- 1 Corinthians 4:7
  Who says that you are better than anyone else? What do you have that you didn't receive? And if you received it, then why are you bragging as if you didn't receive it?

For those who have been stuck in poverty and isolation, you must know that God has always intended that the body of Christ be a significant avenue for support. Many believers proactively give and support those in financial distress, and there are plenty of Christian organisations that have taken this calling very seriously. However, a significant number of believers including those who can afford it, don't make it a priority.

DISILLUSIONMENT AND INJUSTICE

There was a time that I felt an obvious injustice. It's one that I don't like to talk about often, because I realise the differences in scriptural interpretation influences whether it's seen as justice or injustice. It's injustice relating to my gender. I have always served as best as I can, that which I believe God has asked me to do. But evidently some don't agree with the place of women in certain roles. Unfortunately those beliefs aren't always communicated with grace and love, and certainly no argument justifies poor treatment. For a few months I felt that really nasty feeling that gets into your heart when you feel inescapable rejection. I didn't hate the people responsible, and I didn't make a big song and dance about it. But it did contribute to taking me down a path of deep pain and sorrow. But of course, my God came to the rescue. In my reading chair, alone, confused, lamenting, my prayers were honest and raw:

"Why did you curse me by making me a woman?"

"I will never be accepted. Why did you set me up for this kind of exclusion?"

"When will I not be disadvantaged?"

Amidst my tears, I heard the voice of God in a way I can never describe though I have faithfully tried. He said this:

"How could you think that you would ever be disadvantaged, when you have me?"

The relief and healing that came was palpable. A painful cry came from deep in my belly. This one incident represented an acknowledgement that my future would probably always entail some kind of prejudice on account of my skin colour, or gender. However, simultaneously I was confronted with my own misaligned beliefs about the power and influence of the Holy Spirit; my advantage in every way. By believing that the Holy Spirit is powerful enough to raise Christ from the dead, I am also agreeing that He can overcome any barrier that is thrown in my way by humankind. I AM NOT A VICTIM and neither are you. We are overcomers! I am not trapped by man-made rules. We are not ruled by their system, though it feels like reality would tell us otherwise.

Reality is an interesting concept to me. We look around us and see that which is in front of us, and we think we are being wise when we look to reality to define the truth. But if reality is defined as 'what is' and that which exists, then we cannot nullify the spirit realm. As believers we know that there is major activity happening around us in the spirit realm. We know that the kingdom operates on a completely different set of rules. I know it looks like you are at a disadvantage or that your life is targeted in this physical realm, but we must look at what the spirit of God is doing and how He responds to those who are excluded. The scriptures are full of stories where God is favouring the oppressed. Where God is choosing those who nobody else would choose. For His short three years of ministry, He spent minimal time with the Pharisees but He was lavish in His time with social outcasts. Even those He chose to be disciples weren't the pick of the bunch. By looking at obstacles through the eyes of the spirit realm, there are no barriers where the Spirit reigns. Trusting Him, and walking out the plan He has for your life, doesn't guarantee that you will be protected, but it does guarantee that you will be rewarded. Even if that reward is in the life to come.

Will you still experience prejudice? Absolutely! There are people who may reject this book because of some personal traits they have disliked in me. And I'm ok with that if their intent is to be faithful to the Bible as they have interpreted it. Though I expect the same courtesy in my efforts to be faithful also.

Will it hurt? Absolutely! It will probably hurt every time, though I expect I will get quicker at being able to pick myself up and keep going. And when it hurts, I'll go straight back to God and offer some honest prayers and allow Him to be my fortress.

Will their prejudice stop the power of the Holy Spirit working in my life? Absolutely not! And it certainly hasn't so far. In fact, in my opinion every challenge I have faced and endured with a sweet spirit has attracted an unreasonable increase in the activity of God's Spirit in my life.

It does mean that life may be more complicated. I have dreams that I wish to see in my lifetime, that may not be executed as simplistically as it would appear to occur in the lives of those around me. My white Australian husband has worked hard, and been rewarded with opportunities and finances. Nobody asks him or challenges him about how he fathers our child or where our daughter is when he turns up to something alone. This is not my experience. But I can't give up, because I must demonstrate the power of God in my life. My life is a testimony to the fact that no prejudice will ever limit what God can do in me and through me for this world and His people.

My experiences are nothing compared to Australian Indigenous people who have lost their lives in custody, or US citizen Elijah McClain who lost his life by police who abused their power. It's totally different. But as believers, we must reflect every situation we endure back to scripture. We must learn to fight our battles, as He would have us fight them. And just so you know, Jesus wasn't silent in the face of oppressors. Fighting God's way doesn't mean relinquishing your ability to speak up. It doesn't mean accepting the death of Elijah McClain and so many others like him, like it was an inevitable evil. It was WRONG! And you should mourn and lament, and be righteously angry that people use power in such an abhorrent way. And when you feel like the time for mourning is over...heal, forgive, keep your heart sweet, and ask God how He wants you to continue participating in bringing justice to this world.

Let's talk about some particularly difficult thoughts that can lead you down the path of disillusionment, when injustice occurs.

- "It's unfair"
- "They got away with it"
- "It's not my fault, but I'm paying for it"
- "Things will never change"

When someone is able to get away with sinful activities that harm others, we all want to see justice, besides the perpetrator. Created in the image of God has wired us to desire to see justice. Psalm 50:6 tells us that *'God is just'*. Justice is a part of His nature, and therefore it stands to reason that it would also be a part of ours. Thus we shouldn't ignore this part of us, but we ought to also acknowledge that sin can pervert the human view of justice. Sometimes our desire for justice looks like revenge. We want them to suffer until WE are satisfied that they have received the retribution WE think they deserve. That's revenge. I don't think it is necessary to talk extensively about revenge here, except to say that revenge is fueled by hate. And obviously hate is not a Christ-like trait. As with all things, the desire for justice is healthy but in its extreme it is unhelpful. So how do you come to terms with these statements?

Well, firstly for those who say 'It's unfair'. You are probably right! Life can be just unfair. It is unfair when we are limited by the choices of others. It's unfair when people will deal with trauma and hardship because of another's actions. It's unfair that some may struggle to reach their goals in life, because of external factors. Life is actually pretty unfair! The scales can be really unbalanced. Reconcile the unfairness of life with this:

- Acknowledge that the enemy doesn't fight fair
- Know that God does vindicate
- And trust that God has a plan

The presumption, in the Western world, is that fairness and success in life is highly anticipated. We are far less familiar with ongoing hardship, than our brothers and sisters in developing countries. We are actually relatively naive about hardship, and what it is like to have to fight and scrounge for our basic physical needs. Corruption and evil, is not usually observed on a daily basis and certainly not to the extremes that a war-torn country might endure. However, humankind is also capable of incredible good and both believers and unbelievers do good everyday. Naivety about the evil that happens, causes us to be surprised by injustice. Therefore when injustice occurs, we struggle to reconcile this with our faith, because we expected fairness. But the reality is, that the enemy doesn't fight fair. Both the believer and the non-believer are the focal point of the enemy's attack. Don't be fooled, the enemy wants you dead. He doesn't have to physically annihilate you to kill you. The idea that life is fair, is the illusion. It is a child-like notion. Why did I ever think that I would be reserved from hardship? How have I been so incredibly good that I have presumed I would be excluded from that which is guaranteed in life? In fact, the opposite is more likely to be true. If you are doing something good, you're probably going to attract negative attention. It's like Martin Luther. We all hail him for what he did in nailing 95 theses to the main doors of the Roman Catholic Church, challenging the status quo. But he got significant pressure for this action. In April 1521, Martin Luther was invited to a meeting with the Roman Emperor Charles V in which he was pressured to recant his writings. Luther maintained his position and on the back of these discussions was declared an outlaw and a heretic. No minister would ever have knowingly run toward such a declaration and endure the consequences of such a title. Billy Graham, preached the Gospel to more people in live audiences than anyone else in history, and was frequently threatened with assassination. Good deeds do not equal easy circumstances. Sometimes this statement "it's unfair" can indicate that we thought we were entitled to some kind of special treatment. Not always of course. But sometimes. Maybe we think that because we had it hard as a kid, that we deserve better. That God or someone else, owes us. This is the subtle influence of a victim mindset. A victim mindset makes you feel better at the time, but it is one of the most restrictive states of mind you can have. It doesn't do you any favours beside initially helping you survive through a terrible ordeal. But in the long run, you become a slave to it.

Clearly, if you have been through significant racism or sexism, it is not special treatment to want to be treated equally. That is an absolutely valid desire. My intention here is to ONLY address the internal dialogue that can lead us toward disillusionment.

So let's talk about, "they got away with it". It seems that way. At least at the time. But nobody ultimately ever gets away with anything.

God sees, and He sees more than you or I can see. He is merciful to any person who repents, a quality that all of us benefit from. But God is just, although His justice is enacted differently to our sense of justice. For instance, in the Book of Revelation where Jesus is addressing the seven churches He speaks directly to the church of Thyatira. He makes this remark that the one matter He holds against them, is their toleration of the Jezebel. In the next statement, He explains that He has been patient with her to repent. Are you serious?! If I knew that the enemy had infiltrated the ranks through a person who was knowingly, and with intent, leading people astray, my first inclination would not be to be patient to repent. But Jesus is very patient and gives time for the Jezebel to turn from evil.

But when He notes that the Jezebel is unwilling to repent, He informs them of the consequences coming her way. Sometimes we do have to give time for God to be God. Time for him to enact His will, that is perfectly patient and lacks impulsivity. There are truly some battles that are strictly the Lord's to fight. Firstly, we must trust that He will act. Secondly, His actions will be perfect. Thirdly, regardless of what happens His vindication operates for every person who has been treated unfairly when we keep a sweet spirit. In your anger do not sin. Don't gossip. Don't slander. Don't instigate division. Pray desperately. Seek God hungrily. Heal. And forgive. God will vindicate you. Look at the story of King David - read 1 & 2 Samuel and Psalms to learn more. He was hunted like he was a criminal by a delusional king. And yet he was exceptional. It might have taken a while, but God made a way for him to be king. And Joseph! He was constantly being treated unfairly, but God had a plan. And He has one for you too. Those who harm you do not get the final say on your life.

Ok, lastly we must talk about this statement: "It's not my fault, but I'm paying for it".

It is one of the greatest challenges in life, that often the bystander or the victim at least imminently, receives the brunt of the consequences for another's poor choices. When a relative abused you, it was you who then had the lifelong and painful task of healing the associate wounds remaining for a situation you didn't cause. When a church splits because of one person's choice, the whole church feels the pain of that bad choice. When a marriage disintegrates, the children are often left with long term emotional pain. Unfortunately, we often are able to perceive in greater measure the significance of community when a bad situation occurs, when we are able to see the ripple effect of that bad choice. The Old Testament story of Ruth and Naomi encourages the believer who is faced with this dilemma. Naomi and her family were never meant to be in Moab. To abscond when the famine hit, was a sinful individualistic choice at the time. But Naomi had no choice but to follow her husband Elimelek to Moab, whilst he married off his sons to wives outside of his nation. Also a significant no-no. But Naomi was gracious and accepted her daughters-in-law. When Elimelek died, she was left as a widow. As previously mentioned, one of the most vulnerable states she could be in. At least in her own community there was a potential of safety and support, as the Jewish laws protected the widow. So she ventured back to the land of Judah. And Ruth came with her. While in Judah, she had an incredible opportunity of redemption through marriage should she find her kinsman-redeemer. An Israelite law allowed for a widow to be brought under the security of the closest male relative. Boaz filled that role, and both Naomi and Ruth would be safe.

The point of reminding ourselves of this story is to say that Naomi was directly impacted by the poor choices of her husband. She was brought outside of her community, God's laws were being broken AND she ended up alone and vulnerable. None of this was necessarily her choice. And maybe the fact that she was so eager to return to her homeland, implies where her heart always desired to be. It's hard to say, since it is not so explicitly noted. Naomi could have died on the journey back. She could have been attacked, travelling on her own. She could have stayed in Moab; vulnerable to the sin and enslavement that occurred there. Instead she took the risk of journeying back to her home, with Ruth by her side. Two vulnerable women, with no guarantee of a future. And yet God honoured Naomi. He honoured and blessed Ruth. Not only did Ruth have a child, but she and Naomi would forever be in the line of David. Ruth's son became David's grandfather, the family line from which Jesus is a descendant. God often picks those who have been oppressed to do great things in this world. When we participate with Him and respond to His call to heal and worship, He rebuilds us piece by piece with grace and love abounding. Like a crystal that is held up in the light, it streams through each facet, so God desires to lift us up as we radiate His goodness.

Let's talk about "things will never change". When you know that there will always be this trait that influences others' response to you, you may find yourself thinking this statement. It can feel really hopeless. And I wish I could tell you that your situation will change, but that would probably be a lie. The fact is, that cultural change of this proportion is usually incremental and slow. It happens over generations. That which was acceptable in the past is not acceptable now. That which is acceptable now, won't be acceptable in twenty years time. Despite how discouraging this can feel, you must know that God favours you. It may not seem that way, when you experience the limitations imposed by man. But this is a promise. God favours you. While we all do what we can to help the generations change, we aren't really in control of how quickly that change occurs. But the promise that God favours you, can be enough to carry you through this life. And if it can be enough, then I would say that it must be enough. It might be the way it is right now, but I promise you that it's not the way it's going to stay. When the Bible tells us that '*His grace is sufficient*' (2 Corinthians 12:9), it means His grace is all we need and can be relied on for any situation we might find ourselves in. Be encouraged to lift your faith and not let the enemy get you down. Life isn't going to be perfect, but His grace is sufficient.

This quality that others reject you for, that they have decided defines you, is not how God defines you. If this doesn't really encourage you in any way, desperately pray that God will grow your understanding of this grace so that you can see how it can be enough for you.

The one story in scripture that ought to give us all hope is the parable of the persistent widow in Luke 18:1-8. Jesus tells us:

> *"He said: "In a certain town there was a judge who neither feared God nor cared what people thought. And there was a widow in that town who kept coming to him with the plea, 'Grant me justice against my adversary.'*
>
> *"For some time he refused. But finally he said to himself, 'Even though I don't fear God or care what people think, yet because this widow keeps bothering me, I will see that she gets justice, so that she won't eventually come and attack me!'*
>
> *And the Lord said, "Listen to what the unjust judge says. And will not God bring about justice for his chosen ones, who cry out to him day and night? Will he keep putting them off? I tell you, he will see that they get justice, and quickly."*

I find it remarkable that Jesus tells this story about praying persistently, but He uses the example of justice in His demonstration. If you want to see justice, do not lose hope. Pray persistently to your heavenly Father. This is His promise to you in Luke 18:8 *"He will see that they get justice."* He said this. This is His guarantee to all of us.

On a practical note, be encouraged to use the disillusionment inventory featured in Chapter 4. Maybe some of the statements included are not the specific statements you face. The only way to really heal from disillusionment is to break it down as you have observed throughout this book. Because of my particular interest in this chapter, I would encourage you to reach out to me online or through social media. I only seek to help any person who finds themselves stuck in disillusionment, and I realise that this is a really difficult type of disillusionment to face.

There is no real reassurance that things will change tomorrow. But it is possible to have peace and joy in your heart, despite what is happening around you. Let these thoughts help you in your journey.

Apostle Paul

Finally, we arrive at one of the most exceptional men in scripture. Paul is a stellar example of one who walked by the Spirit of God. He is a hero in the faith. We are often taught that he rejoiced in the face of trial, and surely this is one of the most remarkable factors in his journey. However, in 2 Corinthians 1:8 shows a little glimpse that he too has been burdened under the weight of pain and dread:

> *"We do not want you to be uninformed, brothers and sisters, about the troubles we experienced in the province of Asia. We were under great pressure, far beyond our ability to endure so that we despaired of life itself. Indeed, we felt we had received the sentence of death. But this happened that we might not rely on ourselves but on God, who raises the dead."* 2 Corinthians 1:8-9 (NIV)

The theological community has many ideas regarding the specific nature of the trouble that Paul endured in Asia Minor. Some say it may have been a physical affliction, some say it was persecution. For our purposes, it doesn't matter much. Our real concern is the fact that Paul had experienced such significant circumstances and the means by which he endured them. Paul is implying in these first few phrases that he was under a degree of distress that was well beyond capacity to cope with. One theologian notes that the specific language used may have indicated a significant measure of anxiety. In despairing life, he not only believed that his life was likely coming to an end, but that he was utterly at a loss to know what to do. Paul then went on to make this statement: *"we felt we have received the sentence of death"*. The statement implies that the *'sentence of death'* was one that was internal. There was no external entity imposing this sentence.

What exactly does it mean to feel within the sentence of death? Tom Wright, New Testament theologian, suggests that the description Paul gives sounds like a nervous breakdown. He even suggests that Paul may have been hearing a voice telling him to give up and die.

WHAT ARE THE SIGNS OF DISILLUSIONMENT?

When we investigate this aspect of Paul, in its entirety, it would be easy to deduce that a level of disillusionment may have been present. Although we may never know for sure. This despair he describes was far beyond disappointment. His reserves of hope were at an all-time low. He had no vision for how he was going to see through this season. Some versions even use the word 'perplexed'. And although it didn't appear that physical death was imminent, a death within had taken place. It's likely that Paul didn't have words like 'disillusionment' to describe the various modes of emotion. But the presence of depression, confusion and despair make it seem that at least in part that disillusionment had been present.

The exciting fact about Paul, is that his growth through this time of hardship is obvious. He shares with us his conclusions. Paul learns to rely on God as opposed to himself and the capacities within his own human potential. He includes this statement 'who raises the dead'. Whilst Paul had experienced a death of sorts, God is identified as the one who can raise the dead. And so even in death, whether physical or other, we have this hope that God is able to revive. I find this so spectacularly interesting. Not even death is final with God.

He also goes onto say this one statement that I believe, can be an anchor for every person that faces disillusionment:

"We are pressed on every side by troubles, but we are not crushed. We are perplexed, but not driven to despair. We are hunted down, but never abandoned by God. We get knocked down, but we are not destroyed." 2 Corinthians 4:8-9

WHAT CAN WE LEARN FROM THE STORY OF PAUL?

1. We must learn to rely on God

It is arguable that relying on God is the very substance of faith. I have often wondered what 'relying on God' is even supposed to mean. Sometimes it is easier to define something, by working out what it is not. For instance, it is easy to understand how we rely on ourselves:

- Use skills of knowledge and reason to resolve a matter
- Use relationship building skills to negotiate a better outcome
- Look to financial reserves to purchase tools that would equip a move to an alternate situation
- Physically remove barriers to fix a situation, or mitigate the influence of that situation

For most of the situations faced these days, we will employ actions that essentially fall into the above principles. Getting more organised, decluttering, reading books, buying a Thermomix, having an intervention, mediations, getting better apps, taking a course, building a career, using a high interest saver account, taking a holiday...and on...and on. NONE OF THESE THINGS ARE WRONG! In fact, sometimes God is the very one who has provided these ideas as a means to resolve our present pressing matters. These are simply examples of how we can

125

rely on ourselves to fix a situation. However, we all know that there is a point we get to where none of these solutions are adequate in solving the problem. And then we turn to God. This is not the way God intends for us to work. With any of the situations we find ourselves in, we are to turn to Him first. He may not appear to answer. And sometimes that is a sign to wait. And other times that is simply God's way of saying "you already know the course of action". Or get advice. But at least asking Him first, He is invited into the situation. And when He does speak, then that's fairly straight forward. Do as He has instructed.

But relying on God would be to turn all of those coping principles toward God. Instead of simply relying on your own logic and reasoning, ask Him what He thinks. Search His word for His position on your problem. Instead of looking to someone else to fix the problem, pray and ask Him to intervene. Ultimately, instead of looking to external solutions and the strength that is within you to resolve your woes, look to God and what He can do within you by His Spirit to sustain and direct you. Because there has never been a single external quality or entity outside of ourselves that has ever successfully resolved that which we lack. And there is always a limit to what can be handled in our natural capability. In the supernatural it will be puzzling, but it's possible that you will not despair.

2.   Aim your hope

Hope is not some airborne entity that floats independently. It is grounded. It is anchored.

> *"This hope is a strong and trustworthy anchor for our souls."* Hebrews 6:19

Anchors can be very heavy. They are made of materials that are sustainable and hard wearing, and aren't easily broken. And they are shaped with the intention of securing a vessel, and keeping it steady.

The writer is deliberate to say 'this' hope, which suggests that our hope is not in hope itself, but it is attached to a greater strength. That hope is attached to a weighty, durable, and steadfast foundation. So, what is this hope? The fact is that all of us are presently putting our hope in something. At one time, I put my hope in a relationship, my finances, my career, my physical appearance, my talents and gifts…you name it, I have put my hope in it at some time in my life. But were any of these ideas weighty enough, durable enough, and shaped in such a way to sustain me? Definitely not. If they were, why would I have needed to change my hope so frequently over 37 years? Only one thing is sufficient as an anchor - the Lord God Almighty and everything good that we find in Him. What other hope could have sustained Paul and the early church in the midst of persecution? When you are literally threatened by death and cruelty, and fellow believers are being martyred for their faith around you, can anything besides God and His goodness, be truly weighty enough to sustain your hope? The point is, your hope is attached to greatness. If we want to transition through disillusionment, we must redirect our hope toward Jesus.

3. Wait for His rescue, and have faith that it is coming

Paul still needed God to rescue Him. As mature as we become in God, as vibrant as our faith might be, we will still need God to rescue us frequently throughout our life. Paul was no exception to this. Paul reached a point that not even his zeal could rescue him. He got to a place, where there was nothing left within him to see this through. But in the waiting, Paul did not lose faith in God, although he may have lost heart. Because He knew God. He grew in his reliance on God. He trusted Him. And God delivered.

The fact is, that God can rescue you whether you have faith or not. But having faith is still better. It is only by having faith that we are able to grow our faith. You've heard it before, faith is a muscle. It grows by being used. Even if that faith is hanging on by a thread.

CHAPTER 7

Can we prevent it?

Naturally, it would seem that preventing disillusionment would be a valuable endeavour. It would seem wise to prevent anything that could be harmful. Assuming that disillusionment is harmful, which we have kind of established is not entirely true. Saying disillusionment is harmful, is like saying pain is harmful. Yes, pain hurts. Obviously. But it certainly isn't harmful, in fact a lot of the time pain has a greater success in causing growth than even intentional planned growth. However, in both cases pain and disillusionment are also precarious seasons of life. Whilst there is a potential for unbelievable growth, there is also a potential that it leads us away to silent and angry indecision. So are there ways that we as a society are contributing to the disillusionment that people experience? Yes. There are certainly mindsets that our Christian communities are advocating for, that seem to set people up for disillusionment. It is also important to note that there are some people who are somewhat predisposed to disillusionment. I would certainly fit in this category! There are some people who in their seeking for truth, are naturally highly idealistic and yet are painfully aware of the realities and inconsistencies that exist in this world and find it harder to ignore than others. This is not the majority though, and there are still multitudes flocking to disillusionment.

FAITH AS POSITIVITY

In general, as a society we see the merits in positivity. Motivational speakers of the 90's advocated positive self-affirmation post-it notes on a mirror, reasoning that our outlook on life determined not only the outcome we would arrive at, but also the situations. The underlying subtle fallacy that we create our own reality by the perspectives we choose. You can see how this isn't really accurate for us as believers. We don't create our realities regardless of what mindset we have. Our outlook certainly may improve the quality of our experiences, but they don't change or attract a different set of circumstances.

The body of Christ has often perceived faith as simply being positive. But it really isn't. Faith is a hard-wired conviction that God is capable. It may seem like that is a positive statement, but it's kind of neither positive nor negative. It just is.

Positivity according to the dictionary is an optimistic attitude. But faith isn't really an attitude. It can't be. An attitude is the way we think and feel about something. But faith is the substance of our thoughts. It's what we actually believe, not just perspective. If negativity sees the glass as half empty, and positivity sees the glass as half full, faith sees only the GLASS and is unmoved by what is in it, or it's quantity.

The reason why this is really important, is because sometimes the faith we are advocating is not really faith, it's just positivity. Now it doesn't seem like the worst kind of approach to advocate for, and you would be right...it's not the worst. But the nuances of positivity don't necessarily provide for a deep and sustaining faith that endures in the face of suffering. At some point, the circumstances will eventually confound the person who is trying to stay positive. Job wouldn't have survived on positivity in the midst of his suffering, but he did survive on a real faith in God.

Unfortunately, positivity is what is sourcing the 'inspiration' focus of many believers. A brief scroll through the Christian social media world would reveal an array of quotes that are meant to inspire us into living a life for God. But inspiration without conviction, is bound to disappoint. It is a shallow kind of faith, because it's rooted in emotion. It tells me that faith should feel good. I can tell you now, faith does not always feel good. Being faithful can have you rejected, excluded, in debt, alone and without a plan ahead. Just think about it, if I refused to eat anything that didn't taste superbly decadent you would probably be concerned for my health. And yet the Christian world continues to affirm these emotionally charged inspirational quotes, that may not be grounded in truth just so people feel good? How sustainable is a faith that is rooted in feeling good? Not very sustainable. Worse yet, it leads people into disillusion. Here's the ways in which the positivity message delivers disillusionment:

1. It makes people think that they have to be 'up' when they should just be real about their challenges.
2. It makes people deny major character issues that they really need to be dealing with.
3. It makes people begin to wane in their journey, because they feel shame for not being on top of the world.
4. It makes people dishonest with other leaders and people they are accountable to, because they are scared they will be judged for being down and their struggles continue to be hidden.
5. Anyone who might be obviously struggling, is deemed unstable even though they are probably emotionally healthier and developing a more sustainable faith than others pretending to have it together.
6. Any person who is having a rough time figures that they don't fit into Christian community and they often turn to outside friends to deal with life. Worse yet they conclude that Christian community is not truly accepting.

So you see, positivity over genuine faith is setting people up for disillusionment. The fact is, there are so many people in scripture that

God calls righteous who were brutally honest and ugly, in their struggles. Look at Job, Abraham, David, Jeremiah or Peter. And yet they had a faith that would in some cases carry them right into persecution and martyrdom. They had a faith that could cause them to abandon everything, to be obedient to God. Let's be honest, how many believers do you know who are truly willing to give absolutely anything up to follow Him? I don't know many. But the ones I do know, are not negative and they are definitely not positive. They are simply so ferociously committed that they care very little about such categories.

POSTER BOY ILLUSION

I remember visiting one of my cousins throughout the 80's, and each year there would be a new set of posters on her bedroom walls. New Kids on the block, Bobby Brown.... Her room was covered! I think the walls were white before, but who would really have known with the way she redecorated. More than a decade later I visited my niece in America and she had NSYNC, Backstreet Boys and the like!

I've never been a massive poster person, but I presume people put them on their walls because they want to build their identity. That the images promote the fantasy that people are already entertaining in their minds. For the most part I haven't noticed many of my believing friends putting posters up on their walls. Maybe because my friends are around 40 years old. No judgement if you do have posters, it's simply an observation. But even if it is uncommon, Christians do have their own array of socially accepted metaphorical posters on our walls. Of course, we are fairly unaware of it, but it's there and it seeps out in our conversation, language and expectations. Largely, we all have our own individually determined posters. But the influence of corporate Christianity has definitely influenced what we pine for. Some of these 'poster boy' illusions are contributing significantly to the disillusionment others face today in the Body of Christ.

MARITAL BLISS

Marriage can be an incredible blessing. It is wonderful to have someone who is by your side throughout all the various seasons of life and share the good and the bad. There is nobody in my life who has been more faithful to me relationally than my husband. But generally speaking the concept of marriage seems to attract pedestal-like thinking in the Body of Christ. In Christian circles, marriage is elevated to a level that could be deemed idolatry. For starters, it is talked about as the epitome of companionship. As much as I love my husband, I know that he needs more than just me when it comes to companionship and I need more than just him. He cannot meet my every need. Now I know that most people reading this are nodding in acknowledgement and agreement. But even those of us who agree are guilty of parading marriage above all else. Marriage is significant. And with the high rate of divorce, it stands to reason that we should prioritise it. But when marriage is quoted as the primary solution to loneliness, we set people up for disillusionment. It's true God did say that it was not good for 'man' to be alone. But that doesn't necessarily imply that marriage was the only relational format intended to meet that need. The Bible also speaks very highly of friendship, parenting, siblings, and even grandparents. Jesus himself, despite popular culture's suggestion, was unmarried. His relational status was primarily a son and a friend. And the relationship we find in Him is beyond any kind of relationship we could experience here on earth.

I'll tell you how the idea of a singular perfect companion sets people up for disillusionment:

1. It discredits the value of other relationships, and often people exclude other healthy encouraging relationships for the singular.
2. It presumes a life of below par intimacy for those who are probably called to be celibate and single. This includes those

who are trying to faithfully live a celibate life as a same sex attracted believer.

3. Married people can make community very difficult for the average person when they are so insular.

Here's the strange reality. There actually isn't that much in scripture about how to be married or stay married, were you to compare it to other subjects. Our difficulty with marriage in this era, has probably got a lot more to do with expectations. Generationally, we expect a lot more out of marriage. I'm still not certain if that is a good or not-so-good thing. But we forget that our biblical ancestors still negotiated marriage like a trade agreement. Even in the New Testament, post-Jesus' death and resurrection, marriage was arranged. We don't know if they were romantic to each other back then, or whether they had date nights. Despite that, they were still encouraged by Paul to love sacrificially and submit wholeheartedly. Now we choose our partners, in love, and we still struggle to adhere to these directions. All we know is that regardless of the relational intimacy, they were encouraged to be faithful to each other. Now you'd assume that with the freedom to love as we please, that we would be getting marriage right. That the divorce statistics in the church would be really low. But it appears to be quite the opposite. And I think it's got a lot to do with expecting more from marriage than our historical counterparts. And a decreased reliance on friends and family outside of a marriage.

These days we aren't fully ourselves with our friends, and so the pressure for our marital partner to meet our companionship needs increases. It sounds like an oxymoron, but we are basically relationally independent. We get married, and then we reduce our connection with every other kind of relationship we had prior, including society in general. It doesn't really help that influential Christians are frequently posting pictures of their 'perfect' wives and 'perfect' husbands and 'perfect' marriages, often with this retrospective vulnerability which is not real vulnerability people! It romanticises the 'journey' they've been on. Those kinds of imagery are total illusion producers.

Our expectations of marriage are very high. We expect to feel romance forever and consistently. We expect that our partners will stay the same as they were when we married them. AND we expect them to provide us with the greatest and most consistent relational companionship. And our single friends stand by watching us, thinking 'what relational ingrates?!' They would be happy just to have someone to come home to sometimes. I suppose I can't really say that it was never meant to be this way, because I don't really know. But marriage was never supposed to receive more glory than God, and by observation for some couples it does. And marriage was never meant to hit idolatry level! I'm not even sure if it was supposed to trump the Body of Christ. Please don't shoot me, I'm just thinking out loud! Well there is a lot more in scripture about our interactions in the body, than our interactions in marriage. Admittedly, our marital partner is also a part of the body. But surely that would mean they aren't elevated in importance? Look I know I must be freaking people out right now, because you know the priority list goes: God, Family, Church...Was that Paul who said that? I must be confused. I'm sure I read maybe twice in scripture that we are supposed to love our partners. But scripture encourages us to love each other in the body of Christ many, many, many times. It tells us to be devoted to each other in the Body! Now the risk with saying all of this, is that a workaholic Pastor goes home and tells his wife that he needs to be at work even more because the Bible says that we ought to love the church more often, than we are encouraged to love our wives. THAT is not the point here. By the way, loving the church and loving the Body can have two different meanings these days. I'm not talking about the organisation called the Church, I'm talking about the people. Oh, and by the way, you are also a part of that Body so it would also be unwise to run yourself so ragged that you burn yourself out. That's another kind of idolatry. All I'm saying is that scripture is not encouraging us to be exclusive and worship marriage, that is a choice we are making as a society. And people are making poor choices because of how elevated marriage has become, only to walk right into marital disillusionment. Which according to the experts is a significant factor on the pathway toward divorce.

CHURCH BLISS

There are a multitude of published books that study the myriad of reasons for the current generation walking away from church. Interestingly the reasons the 'dones' (those who are 'done' with church but not their faith in Jesus) provide for leaving church are fairly different to the reasons pastors provide on a platform. Church leaders generally point to offence as the primary reason that church members give up on church. I know for myself, that the journey I was on that brought me painfully close to giving up on church altogether was not at all related to offence. It was disillusionment. The church turned out to be something completely different from what I was told it would be. There was a time when church was my sanctuary. A place where I would escape from my unorthodox world. And then I became a leader in church, and church became a battleground.

The reasons often espoused in literature suggests, that the following are key contributors to pastors, leaders and members exiting church, but not necessarily faith:

- Their expectation of community was not experienced.
- They expected the church to be more outwardly focused, but it was inwardly focused.
- They expected to find relationships, and instead they found bureaucracy.

Whether you agree or disagree with these statements is not the point. The question is 'where are they getting these expectations from?'

If disillusionment is often a result of an unquestioned expectation that perceives a gap between the ideal and reality, then what expectation has been envisioned and where is it coming from?

Here are some common unrealistic expectations:

- **Church is the answer to your community needs.**

    To a degree this expectation originates in scripture. So many believers read passages in the Book of Acts, and it generates a vision of family and community that is so distant to what they experience here and now.

    Unfortunately, it is so hard for me to admit this as I was the Small Group Pastor at my previous church…but it is really hard for the Church to meet people's needs for community. The reality is that community is incredibly hard to really achieve today. Sunday services don't always help (particularly if you attend a big church) and most churches know that so they encourage people to be in a small group. But even a small group doesn't guarantee the kind of relationships that really satisfy those deep needs for connection, when they mostly only operate monthly or fortnightly. Here's the challenge; a lot of people can't commit to anything more than that. So yes, it isn't really an easy matter to fix. There are a lot of reasons why community is really hard to achieve, and they come from both individual and societal factors. It's not that we aren't trying really hard to help people connect in church. But in truth, connection is not enough. Real relationships don't just connect in like a puzzle piece. Real relationships mutually transmit care, understanding, interest and time.

    The error exists in the fact that we still think simply 'being around' people is enough. And it's really not. We know people want to be 'known', but often that's really hard to achieve when your relational exposure is approximately 1.5

hours a week. These aren't necessarily situations that are conducive to open sharing nor are those 1.5 hours with the same people. Sadly, I have heard many church members say that they think the kind of church community they desire is only achievable for the people who are running the church. So, when the church uses language that suggests that people will finally find a home it can set people up for disillusionment.

- **Church is missional**

    Of course, when you work on a church staff you truly believe that you are missional and sometimes you can get frustrated that church members aren't bringing people to church. However, for those who are in the 'marketplace', it can be really disillusioning when a church encourages people to invite their friends but doesn't guarantee that it is a place where their friends will feel safe. A classic example: they hear a leader comment on how some guy on Instagram had the most ridiculous tattoos and that people who get tattoos are 'stupid'. The missionally minded church member has been thinking about inviting Fred from work who has some weird tattoos, including a tattoo on his face, and immediately decides that they can't ever bring Fred along to church. They figure that the church is really not as missionally minded as they say they are, if they are going to make a big deal out of tattoos. Amazingly, over the next few weeks Fred decides to come to church. The missional member has already been able to predict what his leader thinks, but the leader acts as sweet as pie in front of Fred. How long is it going to be before Fred finds out that they are faking it? What if he decides to never come to church again over this? Once again, the missionally minded church member decides that church is not authentic in their commitment to the lost. Because for those who are genuinely missionally minded, they are painfully aware that people outside the church don't fit the mold inside the church. And if you are really genuinely missionally minded and you are prepared for the mishmash of people who might come into the church, you can't afford to be put off by unusual qualities and factors. Can we handle the person who uses swear words profusely in the foyer? Could we handle the woman who says she has a one night stand most weekends? Are we prepared for the homosexual couple who have had a baby through surrogacy to come, in search of God?

Most people won't walk into church on their own accord with such qualities, because they preempt that they won't be received with love. But to ask a missionally minded Christian who might be able to predict a lack of reception, it can be disillusioning.

- **Church is about relationships**

Yes, surely this is what church is all about. At least that is what we all presume. I know that the church is supposed to be about relationships, but unfortunately it doesn't always come across that way. For instance, when a conflict occurs in church, people are often shocked and disillusioned that the specific conflict often becomes more important than the individuals involved and the congregation members. That's at least how it can appear. On a much more minor scale, people often serve for years on a team and when they decide to take a break they realise that relationships suffer. We all want to believe it doesn't, and I understand how it happens. But for the individual, it leads to questioning their relational value to those who they shared with. And of course they may feel used. There are actually many different ways in which the idea that churches care about relationships can disintegrate:

- When someone is dismissive about their experiences
- When new people are swarmed on the first night but are forgotten on the second or third
- when leaders are pushed to do more than they want to
- when people are advertised to about the latest program
- when there is a pressure to conform
- when people are judged unfairly
- when relationship is built to get someone to join a team

There's actually a lot of things that can erode trust because people are different in how they interpret what 'relationship' means. Now maybe they wouldn't have so many expectations, if we didn't refer to it as 'church family'. I've heard Christians lament often at this term. Because it connects with this genuine desire to experience a family, and they feel disappointment when they realise that it's seemingly unachievable.

PARENTING BLISS

We have two remarkably different experiences happening in the parenting realm. Either people are so vocal about the challenges that young people are deciding they don't want to have kids. Or, it's so inflated in value that people romanticise it and struggle significantly with disillusionment. 'Parenting bliss' can be disillusioning for others, when parents advocate that aspects of life and even spirituality can't be fully understood unless you are a parent. I know that being a parent opens up a new realm of God being a Father, but it can be disillusioning for people who can't have children, or who are single or the like when we imply that they can't fully experience God without being a parent.

The expectations of being a good parent, and what exactly defines 'good' has also become an incredibly high standard. There are 'parenting rules' about everything: screen time, sugar content, quality time, play dates, extra curricular activities, sleep routines, nap times and many, many, more topics that many parents have a very 'opinionated-opinion'. Parenting is hard. We are all trying to do our best to give these kids a remarkable life experience to help them make good choices. There is an overabundance of information on parenting including risks our children face. But for the most part the average parent already feels underqualified. With the high expectations being set, there could be parents who think that their kids are better off without them. All because they are disillusioned about what it means to be a parent. My parents were pretty awesome, but there was definitely a time when my Dad had so much responsibility at work that he just couldn't be there for us as much as he would have liked. If he had the pressure that today's parents have, he may have given up on parenting.

Abdicating parenthood can manifest in various ways. It can be walking out on your family, it can be detaching from the parenting experience, it can be having just one child, it can be choosing not to hang out with other parents...it can vary. But ultimately we contribute to it when we decide that we must have dogmatic opinions on how to parent and simply must share this with every parent in sight. Meanwhile, the dad who is desperately trying to make sure that he doesn't reproduce domestic violence in his own family because of his past, feels totally ashamed. When will he ever feel good enough? And that's where the disillusionment sets in. When you feel perpetual shame because you feel you can never be a good enough parent, you start to ask questions that are hard to come back from: "Am I even meant to be a parent?" He ends up spending increasingly more amounts of time escaping into work, because he can't deal with the disparity.

This section was intended to give some idea of how we can corporately contribute to another's disillusionment by setting expectations that may not be easy to deliver. Disillusionment to a degree, is inevitable. As a society, we already have pretty high expectations of life. So maybe it is easy to be disappointed when reality spits out a very different version to the image we had. So it's not to say that the corporate message about these areas is an overpowering force and people are defenceless against it. This conversation doesn't necessarily include the ways in which we are currently steering people away from disillusionment. It is important to be reminded that most people want the illusion. They want to believe that the unrealistic is possible. Ourselves included. As a Small Group Pastor in a large church, I wanted to believe that everyone would come to our church and find the family they'd always wanted. Sometimes they did. But I became very disillusioned myself when I realised that it was far more common to find short lived acquaintances, than lifelong friendships.

As we all bounce around from one realm of life to the next, we are constantly receiving, projecting and accepting expectations about how life should be. Few of us stop to ask the question whether particular expectations are: from God or for us to accept. God's expectations of us are very different to our own opinions. His burden is truly light. But His expectations are far less varied. God wants us to love Him and grow in that love for Him, that we might be fully consumed with love for Him and be fully consumed by His love. You can't even begin to love others, until you allow yourself to be loved by a Heavenly Father. When we are trying to meet all the expectations of life, and your relationship with the Father takes a backseat, disillusionment is never really too far away.

It is inevitable that we unknowingly communicate some kind of expectation about how we think life works. The caution is that we ensure that we don't become Pharisaical and add more and more 'rules' to our Christian walk, particularly if they aren't really so clearly noted in scripture. It may seem like wisdom, but it's not what Jesus wants us to do. If you really think about it, Jesus had very few expectations. This is why '*His yolk is easy*' (Matthew 11:28). The Pharisees made it so hard to access God. But Jesus made it so easy. He stripped away all the complicated rules, and brought it back to the most fundamental concepts: Love. Grace. Faith. Compassion. Prayer. Humility. Obedience. Relationship. And then He enriched and enhanced those ideas to demonstrate their robust and intricate depth.

Ultimately, we might be able to prevent disillusionment, were we to realise that our unrealistic expectations often lead us astray. Despite this, disillusionment can still be a formative process that leads to a deeper and more resilient faith.

FINAL THOUGHTS

After being arrested and released by the Sanhedrin for healing the lame man (Acts 3), Peter and John did something that would be deemed unusual for our modern standard of thinking. They returned to the other believers and told them all that had happened. But instead of being afraid, or angry at those who opposed them, or pontificating over the sad state of affairs in society, or complaining about how unfair the circumstances were...they prayed for boldness (Acts 4:29). They weren't concerned with what would happen to them, or at least it wasn't obvious that they were concerned with such things. Their biggest concern was that they would not retreat in declaring the good news in the face of persecution. And when I say persecution, I don't mean people disagreeing with them or calling them names. Persecution in that time was being beaten, jailed, and even martyred for your faith which is still true of some believers across the globe today. (see www.opendoors.org.au) But despite the fate that might have awaited them, they knew the gospel was the greatest news for all mankind. They didn't have any personal agendas like a career, money, or responsibility that convinced them that living, and the quality of their life was more important than the Message. They gave all of that up when they began following Jesus. There was only the gospel. What did they know about the gospel that made them so committed? Because I am at a loss. I know the gospel is good news, but I struggle to abandon all for Jesus. Despite everything He has done in and for me. I struggle to give up my opinions, my personal comforts, possessions and even just my time for the cause of Christ. They knew something deep in their hearts, that I clearly don't know yet. And I daresay many of us are in the same boat. What is clear is that the gospel has to be far greater than we understand, if it is capable of promoting such conviction and surrender in any person.

See, I think the heart of the challenge is this: We have forgotten that this isn't it. Our life is not destined for only today and all that today can bring. We have high expectations of life because we are focused on this world. But this world is not our destiny. Yes we can experience great peace and joy and healing in this world. But it is not in the affairs of this world that we are supposed to be fully satisfied. Often we are so busy making a life in this world, that we forget that our days here are temporary. We are citizens of heaven. Our allegiance and the values of the heavenly realm are of far greater importance than anything we could cling to here.

So in closing, I want to encourage you to pursue the kingdom that does not end. Don't settle for a shallow faith. Let every trial and challenge, including disillusionment, push you to a deeper heart knowledge and faith in Christ. Develop a faith that is not deceived by illusion. That is real, raw and builds a steadfast faith in Jesus. And as we all pursue a deeper robust faith, may we come to discover the truly life-altering power of the gospel of Jesus Christ that is worth abandoning everything for.

BIBLIOGRAPHY

Gutman, David. *Disillusionment: Dialogue of Lacks*. Milton: Karnac Books, 2005.

Menken, Alan & Howard, Ashman, Walt Disney Pictures Presents *Beauty and the Beast*. Milwaukee, WI: H. Leonard Pub. Corp, 1991

Niehuis, Sylvia & Bartell, Denise, "The Marital Disillusionment Scale: Development and Psychometric Properties", *North American Journal of Psychology* Vol 8. Issue 1 (Mar/Apr 2006); 69-83

Wright, Tom. *Paul for Everyone: 2 Corinthians*. London: SPCK, 2003.

Cherones, Tom, David, Larry & Seinfeld, Jerry, *Seinfeld*, Episode 20, Season 4 "The Junior Mint", aired March 17, 1993 on NBC

Christopher Chabris & Daniel Simons, *The Invisible Gorilla: How Our Intuitions Deceive Us* (New York: Crown, 2010), page

APPENDIX
The Disillusionment Inventory

What am I disillusioned about?	What did I expect to see or thought would happen?	What might God have wanted me to see instead?	Why would He want me to see this?	Can this be validated in Scripture?